CHINATOWN, NEW YORK

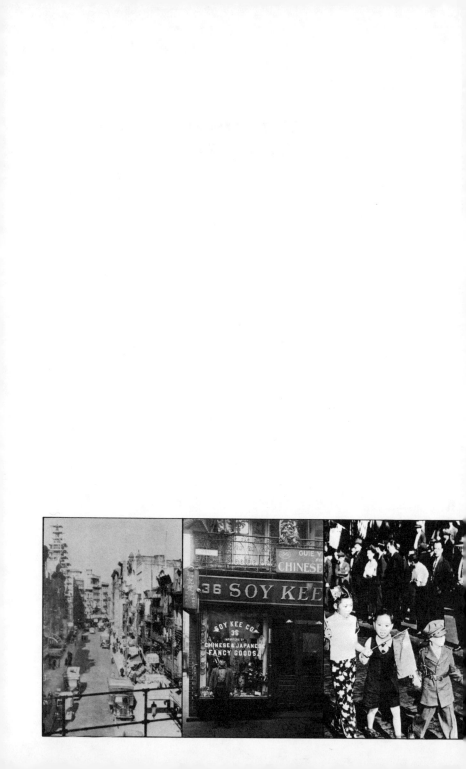

CHINATOWN, NEW YORK

Labor and Politics, 1930-1950

PETER KWONG

MONTHLY REVIEW PRESS · NEW YORK AND LONDON

Library of Congress Cataloging in Publication Data

Kwong, Peter.
    Chinatown, New York.

    Bibliography: p. 165.
    1. Chinese Americans—New York (City)—Politics
and government.   2. Labor and laboring classes—
New York (City)—Political activity—History.
3. New York (City)—Politics and government—1898–1951.
4. Trade-unions—New York (City)—Minority
membership—History.   I. Title.
HD8079.N4K86   331.6'2'5107471   79-2327
ISBN 0-85345-509-0
ISBN 0-85345-526-0 pbk.

Monthly Review Press
62 West 14th Street, New York, N.Y. 10011
47 Red Lion Street, London WC1R 4PF

Manufactured in the United States of America

10 9 8 7 6 5 4 3 2 1

CONTENTS

ACKNOWLEDGMENTS

I would like to express my most sincere thanks to Candia Shields for her tireless efforts in editing and making suggestions on the manuscript. Without her help and encouragement, this book would not have been possible. I would also like to thank others who at various stages provided assistance and suggestions, in particular, Don and Audrey Taylor, Thomas Lim, Kenneth Krabbenhoff, and James Shenton. The countless individuals in the Chinatown community, who were the moving forces decades ago, were kind enough to grant me interviews; they are the "soul" of this book, and I thank them kindly. Finally, many thanks to my Monthly Review Press editor, Susan Lowes, for a most congenial working experience.

CHINATOWN,
NEW YORK

INTRODUCTION

Much of Chinese-American history, like the history of all oppressed groups, remains hidden or has been misconceived. While
there is ample documentation of the discriminatory treatment
meted out to the Chinese in this country, scant acknowledgment
has been made of the popular response and resistance to such
measures. The result has been to perpetuate a stereotype of Chinese
passivity that is very much at odds with historical reality, particularly
in the turbulent years from the mid-1930s to the early 1950s.
This book, then, will attempt to reconstruct the history of the
labor movement in New York's Chinatown during this crucial
period, to recount a story of activism and struggle that has too
long remained untold.

During the Great Depression of the 1930s, many Chinese in
New York banded into labor organizations in an attempt to win
employment opportunities and job security. Traditional social and
political associations controlled by the local merchant elites had
long dominated Chinatown; now new organizations, formed by
laundrymen, seamen, restaurant workers, and the unemployed,
increasingly posed a challenge to the existing power structure. This
labor movement was not, of course, purely a response to internal
conditions. Against the background of the most severe depression
in U.S. history, the U.S. labor movement as a whole had launched
a drive to unionize the unskilled, the minorities, and the un-

employed in a program that had much in common with the ideological and political thrust of the Chinese workers' organizing efforts and was bound to influence them. Then, too, New York's Chinatown received a certain revolutionary impetus from China itself, where progressive forces were struggling to establish a new nation free of feudal autocracy and corruption.

Why the specific focus of the labor movement in Chinatown? Because the overwhelming majority of Chinese emigrants, fleeing oppressive political and economic conditions in their homeland, came to the United States in search of a better future as *workers*. Hence, the history of the Chinese as a group in this country is largely a history of their experiences as part of the working class— but a part so marginal, exploited, and vulnerable to economic fluctuations that no genuine improvement in their status was possible as long as they were denied a freer access into the U.S. labor market. The labor movement of the 1930s represented the first organized attempt by Chinese workers to move into the mainstream of the U.S. labor force and away from the low-paying, labor-intensive jobs—in laundries and restaurants, for example— to which they had been traditionally restricted. This attempt proved unsuccessful, yet its very failure is instructive, demonstrating the crucial role played by public attitudes toward the Chinese immigrants and thus ultimately addressing the reality of the extent of their integration into U.S. society.

In considering this question, the dominant trend in scholarship today has been to emphasize cultural factors; and because such studies view the Chinese community as homogeneous and devoid of internal conflict, the image they project is misleadingly static. This book, in contrast, by stressing the importance of class, is able to show that New York's Chinatown was far from quiescent—that an intense struggle between merchant elite and working people forms a continuous thread throughout its history and constitutes the very dynamic of its political life.

What I am trying to get away from is the all-too-common tendency to use "racial" factors to explain the condition of minorities in this country. To assert that selection and discrimination are a result of pigmentation and physical characteristics is both unscientific and imprecise; it fails to explain the many subtle differences in the way the U.S. social system operates vis-à-vis each racial group, as well as to encompass within its framework class divisions within such groups. Because the nation is the primary and most conscious level of division in the world today, this book will analyze the selection and discrimination process not along racial lines but by taking what might be called a "national" approach.

There is a hierarchy among nations, with the citizens of a strong state, buoyed by the ideology of "national chauvinism," discriminating against the citizens of weaker ones. Applied to the United States, a "national" approach assumes that there will be a close correspondence between a group's treatment in this country and the international standing of the group's homeland. Even an individual who is born here or has lived here for decades still tends to be viewed as a "national" of his or her country of origin; thus, national identity is not merely a symbolic matter but has a real and enduring impact on a group's experience in the receiving country. The fact that China was weak and backward—what many described as a half-feudal, half-colonial society—meant that it was much easier to treat the Chinese in this country as inferiors, just as the unfavorable status of Puerto Ricans is directly related to Puerto Rico's colonial status vis-à-vis the United States. And although physical characteristics obviously play a part in such discrimination, the theory of "race," as opposed to a "national" approach, can only provide a superficial and generalized explanation of a national group's experience. It can suggest why the Chinese in this country have been downgraded, but it cannot explain exactly how and why they were treated differently from—and sometimes better than—other minorities, such as Puerto Ricans, U.S. blacks, or Japanese. For example, even though many consider the Chinese and Japanese similar—both are "Asians"—the actual experiences of the two nationality groups have been significantly different. In the

1940s, when Japan was the "enemy," Japanese-Americans were
sent to concentration camps; China, on the other hand, was hailed
as an ally and the long-standing Exclusion Act against Chinese
immigration was lifted. By the 1950s, China's role in the Korean
war had made Chinese-Americans suspect, and throughout the
Cold War years Chinese communities in the United States were
kept under strict political control.

The ultimate purpose of using a "national" approach in the
study of the Chinese is to encourage its application to other groups
in the United States. Admittedly, such an analysis is complex and
may not be equally relevant to all groups. Nevertheless, if applied
selectively and intelligently, I believe it can sharpen our understanding of the nature of discrimination in this country: for example,
how and why Cuban nationals are treated differently from other
Spanish-speaking Americans, or why the Italians' "ethnic" factors
are more enduring than those of the Germans.

RESEARCH SOURCES

Written material relating to New York's Chinatown during the
1930–1950 period is scarce; still, there is considerable information
to be found in several local Chinese newspapers of the period, and
it is on these that this research is primarily based. The four
newspapers used as major sources range over the full political
spectrum: (1) *Chinese Nationalist Daily (Min-ch'i jih-pao)* (1928–
1938), a conservative paper and chief representative of the official
Kuomintang press; (2) *Chinese Vanguard (Hsien-fung pao)* (1930–
1937), a radical Marxist weekly; (3) *Hsin Pao* (1942–1948), a liberal
but politically neutral newspaper; (4) *China Daily News (Hua-
ch'iao jih-pao)* (1940–1955), a left-wing paper which at one point
had the largest circulation in Chinatown.

As for oral sources, interviews with old residents of New York's
Chinatown yielded insights into the labor movements there, while

the recollections of activists of the period—specifically, leaders from the CIO, NMU, IWO, CP-USA, and many other groups—provided data on Chinese involvement in U.S. labor and political movements. Since any interviewer may lack "objectivity," and since the subjects were being asked to recall events that had occurred some forty years ago, the oral information is used primarily to verify written materials and to help reconstruct events. Oral sources are cited only when written ones are not available, and because of the political sensitivity of the topic, the participants had to remain anonymous.

For more general information, many Chinese and English secondary sources were consulted, including historical texts, trade journals, organizational periodicals, political pamphlets, court records, and even contemporary novels that helped gain an accurate feeling for the period.

1
NEW YORK'S CHINATOWN BEFORE 1930: ECONOMIC AND SOCIAL CONDITIONS

In order to explain why and how the Chinese in New York became so isolated, so ignored by the rest of U.S. society, it is necessary to describe the particular historical conditions that shaped the community. Here I will briefly outline the circumstances that led the Chinese to emigrate in the first place, the conditions that led to their legal exclusion from the country in 1882, and the role the U.S. labor movement played in this exclusion.

WESTERN EXPANSIONISM AND CHINESE IMMIGRATION

Large numbers of Chinese began emigrating to the United States as laborers around 1847–1848, as the result of both "push" and "pull" factors. On the one hand, in the South China provinces of Kwangtung and Fukien a growing imbalance between population and food made living conditions difficult, a situation exacerbated by the devastation and impoverishment that followed the T'ai Ping Rebellion of 1850–1864. On the other hand, gold was discovered in California, creating a need for cheap labor, which, since there was as yet no continental railroad, could be most easily obtained from across the Pacific.

This "push and pull" explanation, while generally correct,

17

leaves much unsaid. It implies an equal and mutually beneficial relationship between the Chinese in need of work and the U.S. employers in need of labor, and ignores the unequal power relationship between China and the Western colonial powers, particularly the United States. This unequal relationship is essential in explaining the unfavorable treatment subsequently experienced by the Chinese in this country.

The large-scale migration of Chinese laborers to foreign lands did not begin until the Chinese defeat in the Opium War in 1842. Before that few Chinese left the homeland, and those who did went mainly for commercial purposes or to escape political oppression. When the Ch'ing Dynasty overthrew the Ming in 1644 and established Manchu rule, many Ming fled to Formosa and South Asia, which they used as a base for periodic attacks on the South China coast. To prevent these expatriates from gaining new recruits and agitating for rebellion, the Ch'ing government forbade any emigration, decreeing that "all those who clandestinely proceed to sea to trade, or who remove to foreign islands for the purpose of inhabiting and cultivating the same, shall be punished according to the law against communicating with rebels and enemies, and consequently suffer death by beheading."[1] Chinese overseas who suffered local mistreatment and abuse could expect no sympathy or support from the government, as was clearly stated in an imperial edict: "You human trash, leaving home, deserting family graves to seek profit, should expect complete indifference from the court."[2]

The intrusion of the Western colonial powers, however, began to undermine the government's ability to enforce its authority. Colonial nations in search of new markets had shown an interest in China as early as the sixteenth century, when Portugal requested permission to trade. China was then a prosperous country and the imperial court, seeing little need for outside relationships, refused. But in 1557 the Portuguese bribed local officials and established a trading post on a small peninsula in South China named Macao; in 1757, the court itself opened the port of Canton to limited trade with foreign countries.

As the Western powers' drive for foreign markets intensified, there was urgent need for a large supply of labor to develop and extract resources from newly acquired areas, particularly the Caribbean and Latin America. Non-European slaves, Africans in particular, were used extensively for this purpose, but in the early nineteenth century, with the outlawing first of the slave trade, and then of slavery itself, other sources of cheap, diligent labor had to be found. After the British conquest of India, East Indians began to appear in British territories as "contract labor"; Chinese workers, however, were not yet available, for China continued to refuse to expand its trade with the West and maintained its strict anti-emigration laws. But China was an agrarian nation, "backward" compared with the industrialized powers of the West, and in 1842 the "closed door" was finally smashed open. The Nanking Treaty ceded Hong Kong to the British and opened five additional Chinese seaports to trade. With these ports opened, the Chinese government could no longer control the movement of its nationals, and its restrictions against the emigration were in effect nullified. Now recruitment could begin in earnest, and between 1847 and 1874 it has been estimated that between 250,000 and 500,000 Chinese laborers were shipped from Amboy, Canton, Hong Kong, and Macao to the plantations of Cuba, Peru, Chile, and the Sandwich Islands alone.[3]

The "coolies," as the Chinese laborers were called (from the Chinese word meaning "hard labor," or, as historian Gunther Barth has called it, "bitter strength"),[4] were recruited by "crimps," who collected from $7 to $10 per head to deliver them to various depots. Often, the laborers were taken as prisoners in interclan fights and forced into signing contracts; they were also tricked into gambling losses and obliged to pay their debts by surrendering their persons, and some were even kidnapped or "shanghaied." No wonder the Chinese cynically called the victims "pigs," and the whole process the "selling of pigs." Conditions on many of the ships in the coolie trade were as crowded and filthy as those on early African slave ships, and the mortality rate was high. When they arrived in port, the coolies were either auctioned off to the highest bidder, or allotted to various employers. Chinese immigrant laborers, in short, were in many instances treated no better than slaves, and their survival rate was no higher. Of the first group of Chinese introduced to work on Cuban sugar plantations in 1847, 28 percent died soon after arrival, victims of the rigors of the voyage and of poor working conditions.[5]

THE FIRST CHINESE IMMIGRANTS

The United States, like Britain, was keenly interested in China. Even before the Opium War, it had conducted a brisk illegal opium trade, and during the conflict it sent a squadron of warships to the Chinese coast in a gesture of support for the British. Soon after the Nanking Treaty, the Chinese were forced to sign the Treaty of Wanghai (1844), which granted the United States all the privileges previously accorded the British and also awarded U.S. citizens "extraterritorial" rights: their activities in China were to be accountable only under U.S. law. The Wanghai Treaty formally launched the unequal relationship between the United States and China.

In 1848, the discovery of gold in California created the need for a large supply of labor in the West; without a transcontinental railroad, however, workers had either to be shipped around Cape Horn from the Eastern seaboard, or moved overland by wagon train. Under these circumstances, it seemed far more practical and financially advantageous to bring in Chinese laborers across the Pacific.

Some scholars have claimed that the Chinese were at first welcomed to these shores, that discrimination against them only began years later, when they started competing with whites for jobs. But early accounts of China by visiting merchants, missionaries, and diplomats had already helped shape U.S. public opinion, and these impressions, writings, and speeches show that the Chinese had an unfavorable image well before the first gold seekers came to California. As Stuart Miller wrote in his book *The Unwelcome Immigrant*, "The majority of Americans who journeyed to China before 1840 regarded the Chinese as ridiculously clad, superstitious ridden, dishonest, crafty, cruel and marginal members of the human race who lacked the courage, intelligence, skill and will to do anything about the oppressive despotism."[6] Such attitudes laid the groundwork for treatment of the Chinese as "exploitable" labor, for emigrants from a backward country that had recently been subdued by the superior powers of the West could never be viewed as equals or truly "welcomed" by the people of the United States.

This can be seen clearly in the conditions under which the Chinese were obliged to work. Mary Coolidge, one of the earliest historians of Chinese-Americans, and others argued that the "coolie" system was not introduced into the United States because its citizens would not stand for it; instead, the Chinese worked under a much more humane "credit-ticket" system, whereby a broker advanced passage money to an emigrant who then paid off the debt after arrival. This may have been true after the mid-1860s; before that, however, the evidence strongly suggests that there was an attempt to introduce coolie contract labor into this country, but that the employers found it a difficult system to maintain.

In 1852, California state senator George Tingley introduced a bill making possible the enforcement of contracts binding the service of Chinese laborers. The bill was defeated, but only after bitter debate. The following year, members of the Chinese Six Companies* admitted that they had imported workers as coolies in the early years of the Gold Rush but, finding the practice un-

---

*A confederation, represented by members of associations from the six major districts in China that the majority of the Chinese had migrated from. The Six Companies, controlled by the merchant elite, governed the social, political, and economic life of San Francisco's Chinese community. For a more detailed discussion of its New York equivalent, the Chinese Consolidated Benevolent Association (CCBA), see Ch. 2.

profitable and difficult to enforce, had discontinued it.[7] And as late as July 1869, a Chinese Labor Convention held in Memphis, Tennessee, proposed to preserve the traditional Southern labor system by substituting Chinese hands for black slaves. As an editor of the *Vicksburg Times* reasoned, "Emancipation has spoiled the Negro, and carried him away from fields of agriculture. Our prosperity depends entirely upon the recovery of lost ground, and we therefore say let the Coolies come, and we will take the chance of Christianizing them."[8]

The early emigrant to the United States was called *gim sen lao*, or "golden mountain uncle," by the people back home, who shared his belief that he could make a fortune in California. This was not to be, as the Chinese soon found out. Since most of the land in California at that time was owned by the U.S. government, the only opportunity for profits lay in the right to exploit that land—to find and mine gold deposits. This right was seen as the exclusive property of citizens of Anglo-Saxon descent; it was extended by courtesy to "assimilable" aliens, but not to the Chinese.[9] They were accepted as menial, unskilled workers—cooks, house servants, washermen—and the best they could hope for was to purchase and rework almost depleted surface mines abandoned by white miners, who could pick up some capital from the sale and move on to more productive sites.

By 1852–1853, the rich surface mines were exhausted and profits were declining. Miners were forced to penetrate deeper into the ground to realize a fair return, and this required capital resources that only large companies could command—and a cheap labor supply that Chinese recruits were well suited to provide. The small number of Chinese that had arrived in 1849 grew to 3,000 within a year, and between 1852 and 1854 a total of 40,000 more arrived.

Forced out of business, the small independent miners turned their resentment against the Chinese who worked for the large companies, beginning what might be called the first wave of anti-Chinese agitation. In 1852, they pressured the state legislature into levying a $3-a-month license tax on foreign miners, and there were scattered violent incidents involving independent miners and Chinese workers. Harassment, taxation, and even outright murder were common; in 1862, a joint committee of the California legislature reported that it had been "furnished with a list of 88 Chinamen who are known to have been murdered by white people. . . . But two of the murderers have been convicted. . . . Generally, they have been allowed to escape."[10]

In the recession of the mid-1850s, many mineworkers were laid off, but the demand for labor picked up when the U.S. government decided to build a transcontinental railroad, and in 1863 work was started on the Central Pacific. The terrain across the Rockies was so rough that it was difficult to secure a constant and reliable supply of white workers, so Chinese were tried, with gratifying results. The railroad company found the Chinese diligent, resilient, and cheap. To assure a steady influx of such labor, Chinese immigration was encouraged. In 1868, the Burlingame Treaty gave the Chinese the right of unlimited immigration into the United States. Railroad companies, with the assistance of steamship firms, recruited thousands of Chinese under the "credit-ticket" system, and by 1868 there were 12,000 of them working on the transcontinental railroads. Thousands more were recruited to build other lines in the West: the Northern Pacific employed about 14,000, and the Southern Pacific's lines, especially in California, were built almost entirely with Chinese labor. By 1870, there were 63,000 Chinese in the western United States.

As the railroads were being completed, the Chinese began to branch out into other areas of economic activity in the West, particularly construction, farm labor, and manufacturing. California historian Carey McWilliams has gone so far as to assert that Chinese farmhands laid the foundation of the now-famous California fruit and agricultural industries.[11] They worked in light industry, such as woolen and knitting mills, in the fishing trades, and in small-scale manufacturing of boots, shoes, and cigars. As they moved into skilled and semiskilled jobs, they appeared finally to be leaving the fringes of the U.S. working class and entering its mainstream.

THE CHINESE AS ECONOMIC SCAPEGOATS

This was not to last, however. In 1873, just as the railroads were reaching completion, the United States went into another economic depression. In the early 1870s, the ranks of California's unemployed—25,000 railroad workers alone—were swelled by a wave of nearly 1 million migrants from the East Coast, forced west by depressed conditions. And if jobs were scarce, land was still more so: giant stock companies had taken over a large number of mines, the railroad companies had received extensive land grants from the government along the tracks, and other areas were held by earlier arrivals. The opportunities available to incoming workers and farmers were progressively limited, yet despite rising unemployment the transportation of Chinese across the Pacific was such a lucrative proposition that the shipping companies poured more and more immigrants into California. In the 1870s, the Chinese comprised about one-twelfth of the state's inhabitants. And since they were all male and able-bodied, they actually constituted one-quarter of the available labor force.[12] Californians accused businesses of encouraging Chinese immigration in order to get cheap labor; they also accused the Chinese themselves of making the situation worse by "cooperating" with the great landholders and railroad companies. Unskilled white laborers saw them as unfair competitors in an already tight job market because they accepted jobs at "inhumanly" low wages. Skilled workers feared being driven out of their trades. And to small businessmen and manufacturers, the low-wage Chinese workers were allies of the large companies, helping them reduce labor costs and so put competitors out of business. The Chinese were increasingly blamed for the economic slump, and a second campaign against them, far larger, more effective, and better organized than the scattered attacks of the 1850s, began to take shape.

The first anti-Chinese movement, twenty years earlier, consisted largely of harassment and punitive actions; the idea was to make life so humiliating and miserable that the Chinese would leave. As time passed, the attacks escalated: beating Chinese was considered a legitimate pastime for whites, and mob violence against the Chinese community was common. From 1871 on, no Chinese was safe either in person or property, and the attack was carried to the courts with a spate of anti-Chinese legislation. One 1870 ordinance required that every house or room contain at least 500 cubic feet of air space, which effectively ruled out all of "crowded" Chinatown. Another made it illegal for any person on the sidewalk to carry baskets suspended on two sides of a pole across the shoulders, the traditional Chinese method of carrying large and heavy loads. A "queue" ordinance ordered that the hair of every male prisoner be cut to within an inch of his scalp. Several laws denied Chinese children the right to an education in the public schools. [13]

Instead of submitting to these punitive measures, the Chinese challenged them in the federal courts. Many were struck down by Reconstruction era courts under the Burlingame Treaty, the Civil Rights Act of 1870, and the Fourteenth Amendment—the amendment conceived originally to protect blacks.

When the anti-Chinese forces saw their efforts on the state level thwarted by the intervention of the federal courts, they realized that a successful attack on the issue could only be waged on the national level. The movement henceforth took on a more organized, political form: countrywide campaigns were mounted calling for the repeal of the Burlingame Treaty, and opportunistic politicians used the anti-Chinese issue to advance their own interests. The Democratic Party's fortunes had declined after the Civil War because of its pro-slavery position, and it needed to regain the support of the working people. Beginning around 1870, the party staged an amazing resurgence, in California and elsewhere, on a platform that featured, above all else, attacks on Chinese labor and immigration. The Republicans were equally quick to perceive the possibility of using the anti-Oriental agitation for their own purposes, and trade-union organizers, too, found the Chinese question useful in rallying skilled white workers. "Anti-coolie clubs" were formed rapidly throughout the state of California by local politicians and union leaders.

By 1876, the Hayes-Tilden compromise, which turned the Southern states over to the Democrats on the condition that the North withdraw all Federal troops from the South, had ended the Reconstruction era, and "Jim Crowism," first directed against "free blacks," began to affect the Chinese as well. Anti-Chinese agitators in California gained a sympathetic hearing in the U.S. Congress, and a House committee investigating the Chinese question recommended their exclusion. In 1882, the Chinese Exclusion Act was passed. It suspended the immigration of all Chinese laborers, skilled and unskilled, for ten years, and prohibited the naturalization of all Chinese already in the United States.

THE EXCLUSION OF CHINESE

The Chinese Exclusion Act was the first—and, as it turns out, the only*—federal law to exclude a whole group of people by nationality. The only previous federal exclusion act, passed in 1875, was intended to keep out prostitutes and criminals other than political offenders. Another law, enacted in the same year as the Chinese Exclusion Act, excluded convicts, lunatics, idiots, and any person liable to become a public charge.[14]

What made the Chinese so uniquely feared and despised that

---

*Since the Chinese Exclusion Act, Congress has been careful to refrain from using racial or national distinctions as grounds for exclusion. Although Japanese laborers were kept out of this country after 1908, no law was enacted against them; rather, they were excluded by agreement with the Japanese government.

they were the only national group thus treated? In the beginning, they were given much the same reception as blacks and Indians. These were the two groups denied citizenship by the same pre-Civil War naturalization law that had extended it to all "free white persons"; they were also the two whose testimony, along with that of the Chinese, was declared inadmissible as evidence for or against whites by a California supreme court ruling of 1854.

During and after the Civil War, as the Chinese arrived in greater numbers, a shift began to occur. True, the Chinese were still linked with blacks in the minds of the public. "No small part of the persecution of Chinamen," wrote Mary Coolidge, "was due to the fact that it was his misfortune to arrive in the United States at a period when the attention of the whole country was focused on the question of slavery."[15] In the congressional debates over Chinese immigration during the 1870s, the issues and antagonisms of the war years remained very much alive, and any question affecting the Chinese was apt to raise the whole complex specter of black liberation. Without a single exception, the anti-Chinese measures were carried in Congress by a combination of southern and western votes.

Yet there had also been some changes affecting blacks that did not benefit the Chinese. In 1863, for example, the California legislature had removed the prohibition against the testimony of blacks in court but continued the ban on that of Mongolians, Chinese, and Indians.[16] And although the Fifteenth Amendment of 1860 extended citizenship to "persons of African descent," it explicitly allowed the extension of the exclusion to the so-called nontaxed Indians, which included Mongolians and Chinese.

More and more, the attitude toward the Chinese took on a character of its own, quite distinct from the view of Indians and blacks. The Chinese had experienced neither enslavement on the plantation nor imprisonment on the reservation. Furthermore, their treatment was not an exclusively domestic issue; any action against them had to take into account the likely reaction of China. This international dimension was particularly important in the post-Civil War era, when the United States began to emerge as an industrial power and play a greater role in world affairs. Thus, not surprisingly, the arguments used in this period to justify discrimination against the Chinese took on an increasingly nationalistic tone. Chinese were considered undesirable foreigners who would never be assimilated into U.S. society because they were uncivilized, tenaciously clinging to old customs and recalcitrantly opposing "progress" and "moral improvement." The Chinese government was perverse and autocratic, allowing its people no freedom. China, in short, was a threat to the U.S. way of life, and exclusion of the Chinese its only salvation. American Federation of Labor president Samuel Gompers went so far as to argue that the "maintenance of the [U.S.] nation depended upon maintenance of racial purity and strength."[17] Others claimed the Chinese had no loyalty to the United States—their sole interest was in making enough money to send home or to enable them to return home, and whatever wealth they produced would not be left to accumulate in this country.

In the twenty years following the passage of the Exclusion Act, six further acts were passed and two treaties negotiated for the purpose of making restriction more comprehensive and effective. In 1888, the Scott Act prohibited the return of any Chinese laborer who had left the United States. In 1892, the Geary Act restricted Chinese immigration for another decade, required that all Chinese laborers carry identification cards, and denied bail to Chinese in *habeas corpus* proceedings. During this period the Chinese government was in a state of near collapse, too weak to make effective protest against the U.S. government's treatment of its nationals. This, in turn, spurred the anti-Chinese forces on to even more aggressive measures: in 1904 the Exclusion Act was extended indefinitely, and in 1924 foreign-born wives and children of U.S. citizens of Chinese ancestry were also excluded.

This escalating series of legislative attacks had the ambitious purpose of eliminating all Chinese from the United States within a single generation; to this end it refused entry not only to any additional Chinese laborers but also to the wives of those who were already here. This meant that many Chinese males in this country, even those who were U.S. citizens (either naturalized before the law of 1882, or born in the United States), were likely to live as bachelors. The only way they could have families was to return to China, marry, and come back alone to the United States—but then they would still be cut off from their wives and children; moreover, under the Scott Act, they would run the risk of being refused reentry upon returning to the United States.

Not surprisingly, the exclusion laws had a grave social and psychological impact on the life and outlook of the Chinese immigrants. One of their effects, ironically enough, was to encourage the very "unpatriotic" attitudes for which the Chinese had been criticized in the first place. Faced with a hostile environment, many Chinese did hope to return to their homeland as quickly as possible and had no desire to stay in the United States, invest their money in its economy, or become involved in its political development.

These acts also led to a large-scale "illegal" Chinese immigration to the United States and the creation of an "underground" in Chinese communities. One of the most common methods of entry was the "slot" system. Under the U.S. immigration law, all persons born in this country are automatically citizens, as are their children—including, under certain circumstances, children born abroad. Thus, if a Chinese could gain U.S. citizenship—as many did following the San Francisco earthquake of 1906, which destroyed most immigration and birth records, making it impossible to verify an individual's status—he could then return to China and claim to have fathered a son, who could also claim U.S. citizenship. The "slot" system soon evolved into a lucrative racket in which individuals paid fees to become the "paper" sons of Chinese-Americans in the United States.

To the legislative exclusion and the general harassment that preceded and accompanied it, we can add a third level of attack: occupational exclusion. This attack, perhaps because it threatened the very reason that had brought the Chinese to the United States in the first place, was ultimately the most effective of all and was to have a lasting impact on the Chinese community.

From the earliest days of Chinese immigration, there was a clear distinction between Chinese and non-Chinese workers. Whatever the diversity of the other workers' backgrounds, their consciousness of not being Chinese was enough to weld them into a bloc, particularly in times of economic hardship. They not only felt threatened from above (employers) and below (Chinese), but believed there was an actual conspiracy between the two. The result was a crusade against the Chinese initiated by the non-Chinese sector of the labor force and supported by other groups—merchants and politicians, for instance—for their own particular reasons.

There are serious contradictions in the non-Chinese workers' rationale for their crusade. True, the Chinese were often preferred by employers, especially the larger ones, not only because they worked for lower wages but because they were "docile"—unlike, for instance, the "rascally" Irish.[18] It was also true that the Chinese were often used as strikebreakers: in 1870, for example, this occurred in several East Coast cities—including North Adams, Massachusetts; Belleville, New Jersey; and Beaver Falls, Pennsylvania—leading alarmed labor organizers to accuse the Chinese of undercutting demands for higher wages and the eight-hour day.

This does not mean, however, that the companies and the Chinese were in cahoots. The employers' "favor" was fickle and short-lived; in fact, they saw Chinese labor as little more than a convenient stopgap, to be shunted aside when it had fulfilled its purpose. The railroad companies did nothing to relocate Chinese laborers after the completion of the railroads or to aid them during the subsequent depression. Moreover, when the pressure against hiring Chinese workers became too great, the employers were quite willing to move on to other immigrant groups—first the Japanese and Filipinos, then the Koreans and Mexicans. Chinese workers, in short, were just as exploited, and by the same employers, as non-Chinese laborers.

Yet for the nascent labor movement the anti-Chinese issue provided a means of rallying workers who otherwise had little to unify them. The non-Chinese population in California during the 1870s had been driven west by a variety of factors. Some were Western European immigrants fleeing political persecution or economic dislocation; others were from the eastern or midwestern United States—skilled workers whose jobs had been usurped by mechanization and the use of unskilled labor, or small farmers pushed westward by the constant encroachment of a more complex and commercialized agricultural system. Politically, too, this was a diverse population, including Republicans with abolitionist or Free Soil sympathies, Democrats whose belief in the work ethic was coupled with notions of racial superiority, and socialists coming with a strong European working-class tradition. Workers were further divided by the relative backwardness of industrial development in this part of the country. Although California boasted the largest land monopolies in U.S. history, most of its industries were still organized as small factories or shops, and most of the leadership of its labor movement was equally fragmented, apt to defend the interests of a particular group of workers at the expense of the rest. And the "rest" came, increasingly, to mean the Chinese.

"Unions" started by white cigarmakers, for example, were in the forefront of the anti-Chinese assault. In the name of "working-class" interests, they organized boycotts of cigars made by Chinese labor and encouraged others to join "in the effort to break down the most dangerous enemy that has yet threatened the interests of the working man."[19] These so-called unions, however, actually represented small independent cigar producers who were being squeezed out by the larger modernized concerns employing Chinese. The promotion of their own new product—identified by a distinctive white label—was their true objective; the anti-Chinese issue was merely a means to that end.

A similar sort of opportunism seems to have animated the career of one of the most rabid and demagogic anti-Chinese leaders of the time, Denis Kearney. His California Workingmen's Party, organized during the depression of 1877, called for far-reaching economic reforms, including the destruction of "land monopolies." But it also coined the slogan "The Chinese must go," and advocated direct acts of violence "to rid the country of cheap Chinese labor as soon as possible and by all means in our power, because it tends still more to degrade labor and aggrandize capital."[20] Employers who refused to discharge their Chinese help were branded "public enemies," while Chinese workers themselves became the targets of threats, mob violence, even murder, often instigated and led by a member of the party. As for Kearney himself, he was an ambitious politician who seemed to have no interest or experience in trade-union movements. He was not a worker but a "small property holder"—though often described as a "drayman," he actually owned at least three drays[21]—and his party used the Chinese as scapegoats to garner working-class support during a period of high unemployment and economic despair. When the depression ended, so did the California Workingmen's Party.

A more sustained brand of leadership came from the craft unions, perhaps the most powerful force in the anti-Chinese crusade. This has a certain logic, since occupational exclusion was a key principle of craft unionism. As historian Alexander Saxton put it in his book *The Indispensible Enemy: Labor and the Anti-Chinese Movement in California*: "Economically rather than politically oriented, the craft unionists and their leaders sought to maximize bargaining power through union-controlled competition for skilled jobs. To this purpose they strove to define the limits of each craft, to restrict entry by means of rigorous apprenticeship and hiring."

The 1870s heralded a period of rapid growth for the craft unions, and they found the anti-Chinese issue an effective organizing tool.

However minimal the actual threat, the specter of Chinese encroachment on such skilled trades as cigar and shoe manufacture initially served as the single most powerful means of unifying skilled workers into unions. The craft unions' anti-Chinese campaign also enabled them to forge coalitions with the Democratic Party and other groups that controlled California politics; hence, their influence came to extend far beyond a few members in particular trades. Soon the unions were able to deal with employers from a position of commanding power, power achieved on the backs of the Chinese workers.

The anti-Chinese crusade also helped the white craft workers to decrease competition in the skilled trades. If the Chinese were forced into menial and unskilled occupations, the unskilled white job seekers were less likely to come to California. At the same time, the craft unionists singled out the Chinese as the cause of the unskilled whites' joblessness, thus warding off their demand to enter the skilled trades. The anti-Chinese movement, therefore, enabled the craft unions to influence the unskilled workers without having to assume any responsibility for getting them jobs. It became their means of manipulating the political and organizational energy of the entire labor force, ultimately making their leadership and their control of unionized occupations virtually immune to any challenge from the unemployed or the unskilled. The Chinese truly became the craft unions' "indispensable enemy."

Beginning in 1870, the craft unions repeatedly called for expulsion of the Chinese. In that year, the National Labor Union advocated total exclusion, while in 1874 the Industrial Congress and Industrial Brotherhood "opposed the importation of Chinese and other servile workers" and demanded the repeal of the Burlingame Treaty. Among East Coast workers agitating for an eight-hour workday, there were also frequent calls for an end to Chinese immigration.[22] In April 1880, delegates from forty labor unions met in San Francisco and established the League of Deliverance, aimed at ousting the Chinese from their jobs and keeping them out of the country. Before long, the league had thirteen branches and a membership of 4,000 in California alone; it persuaded merchants and consumers to boycott goods made by Chinese workers and pressured factories to discharge their Chinese employees.

Even following the passage of the Chinese Exclusion Act in 1882, union activities did not cease. Although the act barred any further increases in the number of Chinese workers, it did not address itself to the more than 100,000 already in the country. With the depression of 1882, rising unemployment put labor leaders and politicians under growing pressure to give some direction to the discontent of both organized and unorganized workers. Once again, the anti-Chinese issue was used by the trade unions, under the national leadership of the Knights of Labor, to divert the unemployed from their demand that the craft unions be opened up. This time the unions called for the physical removal of the Chinese and their belongings from their homes, and there were many instances of savage violence. In Rock Spring, Wyoming, some thirty Chinese were killed by white miners in 1885; similar incidents occurred in Eureka, California, and Tacoma and Seattle, Washington, where in 1886 the entire Chinese population was driven out by force. As a result, many Chinese deserted these towns and smaller cities for major metropolitan centers, where a degree of law enforcement existed for their protection.

With the disappearance of the Knights of Labor in the early 1890s, the leadership of the anti-Chinese movement passed to the newly organized American Federation of Labor (AFL). A resolution at one AFL convention declared that the Chinese had brought with them "nothing but filth, vice and disease," adding that "all efforts to elevate them to a higher standard have proven futile."[23] Spurred on by the impending expiration of the exclusion laws in 1902, the AFL sent a memorandum to Congress in favor of a new exclusion act. "The free immigration of Chinese would be, for all practical purposes, an invasion by Asiatic barbarians, against whom civilization in Europe has been frequently defended," stated a pamphlet by AFL president Samuel Gompers. "It is our inheritance to keep it pure and uncontaminated, and it is our purpose to broaden and enlarge it. We are trustees for mankind."[24]

It is easy to see that the language of these attacks justified assaults not only on the Chinese but also on blacks and other "undesirable" minorities. And in fact, the craft unions' exclusion of Chinese workers was to serve as a model for their treatment of other racial and national groupings.

So long as the United States remained a largely agricultural country, the excluded peoples, blacks and Indians, could be exploited in isolation, within such closed institutional structures as plantations and reservations. But with the advent of large-scale industrial production and urban settlement, these solutions were no longer viable. The new context required different methods of creating a "docile," uncomplaining labor force, and the Chinese arrived on the scene just in time to serve as the subjects of an experiment. First, they were made vulnerable to a very high degree of exploitation; second, they were kept separate from the rest of society, physically isolated within Chinatowns and politically excluded by the denial of citizenship. Thus, no one had to take responsibility for them when their usefulness as workers ended, while they could be denied many of the rights accorded U.S. citizens.

As we have seen, their development as a "new breed" of menial workers barred the Chinese from trade unions, forced them into unskilled jobs, and kept them outside the mainstream of working-class life. And the unions went on to justify the exclusion of black workers on the same grounds they had used with the Chinese, citing their "readiness to serve as strikebreakers, because of their abandoned and reckless disposition," and their lack of "those peculiarities of temperament such as patriotism, sympathy, sacrifice, etc., which are peculiar to most of the Caucasian race. The best solution would be to export them to Liberia or Cuba."[25] As long as the trade unions depended on the exclusion of particular groups of workers to maintain their ability to bargain effectively with management, such racist and chauvinistic attitudes persisted. While Chinese workers were the first to be systematically excluded, they were followed by the Japanese, by blacks when "free slaves" began to migrate to northern industrial cities just before World War I, and then by Mexicans and Puerto Ricans.

This occupational exclusion did the Chinese even more damage than the immigration laws, for it not only drove them out of the skilled trades but deprived them of any access to industrial jobs. Although most were workers, they had no allies among the rest of the working class and were thus effectively segregated from U.S. society. This situation continued during the 1920s and 1930s, and in some cases persists today.

CHINESE REACTION AND ADAPTATION TO EXCLUSION

On first being faced with the exclusion policy, the Chinese in the United States seemed to believe there might be some legal recourse. When the Geary Act of 1892 required all Chinese to register and submit to identification procedures, including "mug shots," or pay the penalty of imprisonment and deportation, outraged Chinese community leaders advised a refusal to comply and contested the act in court. The Supreme Court, however, pronounced the law constitutional, and immigration authorities threatened to deport those who refused to register. The Chinese then mounted another challenge, but in *Fong Yue-ting* vs. *United States* the Supreme Court ruled that deportation need not be punishment for a crime but could be simply an administrative procedure for returning undesirable aliens to their home countries.[26] Nonnaturalized aliens in the United States were thus in effect denied any legal protection. Since most Chinese were ineligible for citizenship, they could be deported for the slightest provocation; hence, they were understandably reluctant to risk "open" or "active" political involvement.

The Chinese, then, could expect no help from the U.S. authorities. Nor was any help immediately forthcoming from their home government, then on the brink of collapse. Still, they cherished the hope that social and political changes would eventually transform China into a strong nation that could protect them, and as chauvinistic attacks against them mounted, they too became increasingly nationalistic.

In 1905, this patriotic fervor was given a tremendous boost by a boycott of all U.S. goods in China. Organized by merchants, intellectuals, and workers, the boycott began in Shanghai and soon spread to other major cities, showing the depth of accumulated anger and frustration at the way the Chinese had been treated in the United States. Although Chinese in the United States did not openly support the boycott, they were spiritually and financially committed to its success. After a year, heavy losses forced the merchants to drop out, but the students and the press not only continued the ban but produced a wave of anti-American books and periodicals describing the sufferings of Chinese emigrants.[27] The boycott ended only when the Ch'ing court, under pressure from the U.S. government and alarmed at the possibility of a mass uprising similar to the Boxer Rebellion (an antiforeign movement that had brought on an attack on China by the imperialist powers that nearly caused the collapse of the Ch'ing Dynasty), issued an edict to suppress it. Even if the government was weak, however, there was evidence that the people were awakening, and the Chinese in the United States were encouraged to support political causes at home.

Many individual adjustments were also required of the Chinese in the United States. Most of them did not begin from a position of strength, having been uneducated peasants or menial laborers before they came to the United States. Few spoke English, and many never had the time to learn it. Often they started working as soon as they disembarked, constrained by the twin financial burdens of debts incurred by the trip across the Pacific and the need to send money back to support their families in China. In their first adjustment, which was occupational, they were forced out of the regular labor force and had to look for new kinds of jobs, and found their options severely limited. They had little capital, yet wanted work that would avoid dependence on either white employers or workers. Service jobs—as laundrymen, domestic servants, workers in Chinese restaurants—fitted these requirements. Laundries, for instance, could be opened without much capital yet demanded minimal contact with the wider society. Once the first Chinese began to work in these areas, others followed, and they became "Chinese" trades. Thus by 1930, 84 percent of the Chinese gainfully employed in New York were in either restaurant or laundry work.

The second major adjustment the Chinese had to make was geographical. When anti-Chinese sentiment deepened on the West Coast, the Chinese dispersed throughout the country, hoping to make themselves a less visible target, as well as to avoid competition with other Chinese in the narrow range of occupations available to them. In 1880, 83 percent of the Chinese resided on the Pacific Coast; by 1900 the figure had dropped to 66 percent; by 1920 to 55 percent.[28]

It was during this period that Chinatowns began to spring up in the major cities of the Midwest and along the East Coast. In 1880, New York was already reported to have a Chinatown with a population of 800 centered around Mott, Pell, and Bayard streets. In 1940, an unofficial count of 40,000 made this one of the largest Chinatowns in the United States, second only to the one in San Francisco.

CHINATOWN: THE TRADITIONAL STRUCTURE

From 1910 to 1950, the Chinese in the United States lived through an era known as the "silent years," or what sociologist Stanford Lyman called the period of "accommodation," when "interracial antagonisms were inhibited and intergroup conflicts were reduced to a latent potentiality."[29]

True, as far as U.S. society in general was concerned the

Chinese were practically a forgotten people until 1943, when Congress finally repealed the Chinese Exclusion Act. Yet there was a great deal going on inside Chinese communities during this period, particularly in New York.

For the people of New York's Chinatown, these were years of great economic hardship, forcing them to wage a continual struggle to defend their trades against destruction by outside forces. Yet they were not wholly isolated and even found some allies among the labor and political movements of the day. These struggles, however, did not really come into their own until the 1930s. Before that time, traditional organizations dominated, and no effective movement could arise without first confronting this entrenched power structure.

Virtually all Chinese who emigrated to the United States before World War II came from one of the seven districts in the South China province of Kwangtung (which is about the size of the state of Connecticut). The internal social and political structure of all the Chinatowns was a virtual replica of that of the home province, with place of origin and kinship relationships remaining as crucial in the United States as they had been in China.

People who belonged to the same *tsu*, or clan (i.e., those related by blood within an extended family) were considered closest; beyond them came people from the same village. Since individuals from the same clan rarely migrated together, it was often the next order of relationships—people from the same village—that became the primary tie in Chinatown. Tsu members and the people from a village would informally join together into a social and mutual-assistance group called a *fong*, which could have anywhere from twenty to one hundred members. A rented apartment served as its headquarters, as a weekend recreation center, and as a shelter for homeless or unemployed members. Expenses were covered by a membership fee. The fong's main function was to act as a mutual-aid society through which members could inquire about jobs, find partners for joint ventures, and pool or borrow funds needed for new businesses.

The village association *(tung hung woy)* included different fongs whose members came from the same village and had functions similar to those of the fong but on a larger scale. It collected relief funds for victims of flood, famine, or other emergencies in China; it raised money to build schools in the home village or buy arms for its defense against bandits in times of political unrest. It is through the village associations that New York's Chinese kept in touch with what was going on back home.

Above the village associations and fongs, which were voluntary organizations, were two organizations that had a somewhat different basis. The family, or surname, associations *(kung saw)* included anyone with the same surname, which meant that members could come from different villages. The district associations *(hui kuan)* included people from the same district (the lowest administrative unit of the Ch'ing government), or people who spoke the same dialect. Membership in these was not a matter of personal choice. Every person of a given family name, and every person born in a given district, was automatically a member of the appropriate association. Both of these organizations were more remote from their members than the fongs and village associations. While they, too, performed mutual-aid and benevolent work, they were much more oriented toward business and administration. Many businessmen in Chinatown formed alliances with fellow association members in order to gain an advantage over their competitors. (And since everyone automatically belonged to one family and one district association, the choice of which to be active in was based on personal advantage.) On the other hand, when conflicts arose among fellow members, the associations often served as arbitrators. They also acted as representatives of their members in dealing with other associations and with white society—as, for example, in cases of conflict between a member and an outside party.

In short, the "formal" internal structure of Chinatown had two tiers, the bottom one consisting of fongs and village associations, and the top composed of family and district associations. The bottom tier responded to the individual, natural needs of its members and dealt with matters of immediate concern; the top tier, in contrast, arose out of the necessity for regulating different interests within Chinatown as well as for providing community representation vis-à-vis the outside world.

This structure, however, was not as functional as it seemed. Its organizational model, after all, was the feudal China of the Ch'ing Dynasty, whose self-sufficient rural economy was scarcely comparable to the urban industrialized setting of New York's Chinatown. The traditional associations were run on strict hierarchical lines; they demanded unquestioning obedience and total control. Membership, as we have seen, was mandatory, and so was the payment of dues—a member whose dues were in arrears could expect no help from the association. Further, no business transaction was considered legal without recognition from, and registration with, an association.

But although the associations claimed total jurisdiction, they gave something less than total representation: their leaders were individuals of "fame, property, or education," usually wealthy merchants, while the working poor, the majority, were excluded. Further, since only elders were considered eligible, this ruling elite reflected the conservative and traditional bias of older men.

The most serious deficiency of the traditional organizations, however, was the chronic rivalry among them, and therefore their inability to provide stability within the community. There were attempts to set up "spheres of influence"—each association staking out a particular "territory" or a certain type of trade guild—but because Chinatown was small and crowded, any minor shift in jurisdiction altered the power balance. It was to minimize this problem that a federation of family and district associations, the Chinese Consolidated Benevolent Association (CCBA), was founded. Not only did the CCBA act as mediator for intra-association conflicts, but it became the external representative for all Chinatown, known to outsiders as its "city hall." The CCBA was not a panacea, however, and when negotiations failed, open warfare would result, often polarizing the whole community.

The associations, unable to cope with their internal conflicts, were even less able to deal with the emergence of the tongs. These secret societies had been founded by opponents of the Ch'ing regime in seventeenth-century China. By the mid-nineteenth century, they had lost much of their political content but retained their clandestine fraternal nature; in New York, two such tongs are known to have existed as early as the 1890s. Tongs attracted those whose own district or family associations were too weak to protect their members from virtual economic exclusion by the larger organizations. They at first restricted their operations to such illegal activities as prostitution and gambling, and the sale of opium. They also provided a "cover" and a means of economic survival for thousands of illegal Chinese emigrants.

The power of the tongs grew with the profits from their illegal and underground activities, and they began to encroach on the territory of the regular associations. Conflicts resulted, but the tongs had a distinct advantage: their members were bound together by oaths of allegiance, they had a standing army of "hatchetmen," and, being secret societies, no one was sure who their members were. As more and more individuals joined tongs to protect their own interests, these societies became a focal point of Chinatown politics—indeed, association and tong affairs were often indistinguishable. The tongs' characteristically violent methods of resolving disputes—such as kidnappings and assassinations—became the norm, and their illegal operations were considered as acceptable as any other form of business. Ultimately, they were even made standing members of the CCBA.[30]

Starting in about 1910, New York's Chinatown was periodically plagued with the "tong wars." Each crisis was graver than the last, reflecting the breakdown of institutional authority and playing havoc with the lives of ordinary individuals. The normal conduct of business was repeatedly disrupted by outbreaks of violence,

innocent bystanders were forced to take sides, and both the associations and the tongs increased their dues and extortion payments in
order to finance their wars.

The crisis was due not only to the shortcomings of the traditional
structures but also to the exclusion of the Chinese and their
isolation in urban enclaves. Many of the tongs' most lucrative
operations—not only illegal immigration, but drugs, prostitution,
and gambling—played on the desires of lonely and frustrated men
seeking oblivion or lost in dreams of quick riches. The seemingly
meaningless internecine "tong wars" thus have to be seen in the
larger context of the restrictions imposed on the Chinese. Given
the severe limitations on the areas of economic activity open to
them, the commercial expansion of any one tong or association
automatically meant another's loss. Friction of this nature led
to war.

One example of the way these restrictions affected activities was
the practice of *p'o tai*—literally, "store foundation"—a term re-
ferring to the fee a store tenant leaving a business location expected
to be paid by his replacement, even though he did not own the
location. The rationale was that the next tenant would benefit from
the business' established clientele and the "good will" of the
location, and so should make good the former tenant's future loss.
This system was rigidly enforced by the associations (family, district,
tong, and CCBA); and though many Chinese proprietors were
reluctant to pay the fees, they had little choice: because of their
limited choice of location, it was almost impossible for them to rent
where there had been no Chinese business before.

There was to be no substantial improvement of conditions in
the Chinese community until the late 1920s, when dramatic
economic and political changes in the United States began to
create new opportunities. At the same time, the rapid advancement of political reform and national self-awareness in China itself
also had a positive impact.

External events, however, only provided the conditions for
change; there also had to be movement within Chinatown. As

long as an antiquated and traditional power structure held sway, mobilization was difficult. It was not until new labor and political organizations arose within the community that things began to change for the Chinese working people.

2
POLITICAL AND LABOR MOVEMENTS: THE EARLY YEARS, 1919-1930

THE KMT AND THE RISE OF ORGANIZED
POLITICAL MOVEMENTS

The dominance of the traditional associations inhibited the development of organizations based on new principles; hence, the political leadership for change and reform came initially not from within New York's Chinatown but from China itself.

The 1911 revolution in China did not bring about a viable political system but plunged the country into more than a decade of warlordism, with ambitious military leaders vying for power. The Chinese people experienced untold suffering, and the nation was even more vulnerable to threats of foreign aggression than before the revolution. This period of Chinese warlord anarchy coincided with the "tong war" era in New York's Chinatown.

After World War I, however, China embarked on a process of national reawakening, beginning with wholesale re-evaluation of traditional values and institutions. First, in the May 4th Movement of 1919, intellectual elites challenged the narrowness of Confucian conceptions, and of family and clan loyalty, and began to campaign for the cause of national salvation. The political system was analyzed and compared to Western models. The contribution of workers and peasants to society began to be recognized. This wave of intellectual questioning led to practical political movements. Socialist, anarchist, liberal-democratic, and communist parties were founded; the labor movement grew rapidly, and workers began to strike for their rights.

At the same time, the recent successful socialist revolution in Russia stirred a great deal of interest among the Chinese, particularly given the humiliating treatment they had received from the major Western powers and Japan at the Versailles Conference following World War I. Lenin's call for an alliance between communist parties and bourgeois-democratic movements in the dependent countries attracted Kuomingtang (Nationalist Party, or KMT) leader Dr. Sun Yat-sen, whose organization had failed repeatedly in its attempts to transform and unify China. Sun, whose forces were barely in control of Kwangtung province, accepted Soviet assistance and turned his party in a completely new direction.

In 1924, at its First Party Congress, the KMT took a firm stand against warlordism and imperialism, and reorganized along the lines of the "democratic centralist" structure of the Communist Party of the Soviet Union. The congress mapped out three major policies: (1) alliance with the Soviet Union in foreign affairs; (2) collaboration with the Chinese Communist Party in domestic affairs; (3) creation of a base among the workers and peasants. The KMT was transformed from an elite party of leaders into a party of the masses. It began to direct its appeals to a broad cross-section of the population, and party cadres were trained to propagandize among the masses and organize them into political movements. Many Chinese saw the reorganized party as the first real hope for national unity, and its membership and strength grew rapidly.

Overseas Chinese also greeted these developments with enthusiasm. After all, Kwangtung, the party's geographical base—and Sun's birthplace—was the home province of most of them. Moreover, Sun himself was no stranger to the Chinese in the United States: earlier, he had actively solicited their support for his revolutionary cause by traveling to many communities around the country, and in 1921 he even set up a special Overseas Chinese Affairs Bureau within the KMT.

The operations of the "new" KMT had a considerable impact on patterns of political involvement among overseas Chinese. The party set up a branch office in New York and began systematic recruitment of cadres. It attempted to gain support through propaganda and mass organizing. Several party newspapers were established in order to promote the new principles and influence political opinion. This kind of activity was new to New York's Chinatown, which had never had an influential political organization that was not subordinated to the traditional associations.

The newly organized KMT actively spread the party's anti-imperialist and antifeudalist programs and enlisted financial and spiritual support for the party's activities in China. For example, New York's Chinese contributed extensively to the Northern Expedition of 1927, which ultimately led to the nominal unification of China under the KMT. In 1928, the party mobilized thousands to demonstrate against the Japanese massacre of Chinese citizens in the city of Tsinan. Political study groups were formed to learn about developments in China.

After the successful Northern Expedition, Chiang Kai-shek, who had assumed the KMT leadership with the death of Dr. Sun, gained the support of the landlord and merchant classes, and decided to end the Nationalist Party's coalition with the Communists. Chiang set up the Nationalist government in Nanking and drove the Communists underground. He repudiated many of the party's social programs, "postponed" the enactment of reforms, and instead emphasized social "order" and "constitutionalism."

With Chiang's occupation of Peking in 1928, all of China came nominally under Nationalist control, and in October the Organic Law of the National Government of the Republic of China was proclaimed. Noted China scholar Lawrence Rosinger observes that the one-party regime thus established was very much at odds with the democratic practice and theory espoused by the KMT in its earlier years. The government's rationale was that the Chinese people had to be prepared for self-government through a period of "political tutelage." All opposition groups, including Communist and popular movements, were suppressed. According to Rosinger, the "KMT was therefore transformed into a party consisting chiefly of officials, persons wishing to enter the government service, and representatives of the dominant economic groups."[1]

The transformation of the KMT at home affected its overseas branches. In its early days, the KMT had politicized the Chinese community in New York; many individuals had begun to take a different view of Chinatown's own problems and of the need for change. Now, however, there was a wholesale purge of left-wing elements and the emphasis was no longer on politicizing the overseas population but on educating them to preserve traditional Chinese culture. To the KMT, Chinatown became chiefly a source of financial support and investment in Chinese industries, and so the party tended to cultivate the wealthy, influential elites and the traditional associations rather than the general population. The popularity of the party declined in the wake of these policies, particularly among young people, and those who remained were primarily career bureaucrats. The party branch in New York became rife with cliques and intrigues supporting different politically ambitious leaders: one faction supporting Chiang, another backing Wang Ching-wai, a "liberal,"* and a third following Hu Han-min, an arch-conservative. Three "party" newspapers represented the three factions in New York.

The leftists who had abandoned—or been forced out of—the KMT comprised a complex group. They had formed a coalition of various political types, including adherents of the Chinese Communists, trade unionists, and simple patriots. Some were students; others were workers. All agreed, however, that Chiang had betrayed the party by reversing the course mapped out at the 1924 party congress, and were thus committed to the ideals established there. They were not necessarily clear about a program, however. Most had joined the party after 1925 and so had not been

---

*Wang Ching-wai had established a non-Communist but left-wing "counter-government" in Wuhan; in 1928, however, he defected back to Chiang, and years later he headed the Japanese puppet regime in China.

active members for very long; they were highly motivated but ideologically unsophisticated. Much of their time was spent discussing developments in China rather than putting their ideas into practice in their own community.

In 1927, when the leftists were forced out of the KMT, they were still in the process of seeking political clarity. In order to gain a better understanding, many turned to the U.S. left—socialist, communist, and social-democratic—and labor movements, which eventually steered them toward broader social concerns. Some became active in the Red International Union, some in the Communist Party, some in the anarchist movement supporting the cause of Emma Goldman, and some were known to have connections with Trotskyite organizations.[2] But because of their newness to the movement and their lack of practical experience, the Chinese left tended to discuss issues abstractly and adhere to positions dogmatically. As a result, the left-wing elements in New York had great difficulty in organizing into a single group.

Unity was a common problem among Chinese leftists in the United States. The first attempt to resolve it, however, came not in New York but in San Francisco. There, an organization called the Grand Revolutionary Alliance of Chinese Workers and Peasants (ACWP) was formed to oppose the KMT, but it never became more than a loose coalition of leftist forces. A branch of the alliance was started in Philadelphia's Chinatown, where the left dominated the local KMT. After extensive discussion, its members concluded that "both the Nanking government under Chiang Kai-shek and the Wuhan regime under Wang Ching-wai are traitors of the people and the revolution."[3] The party branch was dissolved and a chapter of the ACWP established instead. The members confiscated the party treasury and used the funds to publish a monthly journal, the *Chinese Vanguard*. The early members of the Philadelphia ACWP were a mixture of party functionaries and intellectuals: the organization was a coalition effort, united on the general principles of opposition to the KMT. Few details of its activities are known, but it is reported that there was a campaign to get Chinese seamen to disassociate themselves from the KMT "official" seamen's union, called Lien Yi. [4]

For a while, then, Philadelphia was the center of Chinese leftist activities in the United States. In 1929, however, the scene began to shift to New York, where the combined impact of external developments and internal struggles was accelerating left-wing activities. The domestic and foreign policies of the Nationalist government were creating much apprehension in China. By 1930, Chiang's feuds with various warlords, and his massive "Bandit-Suppression Campaign" against the Chinese Communists, had plunged the country into a state of civil war. At the same time, Japan was readying a full-scale military invasion of China. Several "incidents" were engineered to test the Chinese response, yet the position taken by Chiang was "first pacification, then resistance." The Philadelphia ACWP, appalled at this nonresistance to Japanese imperialist policy, changed the name of its organization to the Chinese Anti-Imperialist Alliance and moved both its headquarters and newspaper to New York.

THE CHINESE ANTI-IMPERIALIST ALLIANCE

The establishment of the Chinese Anti-Imperialist Alliance in New York ushered in a new and more active era for the Chinese left. It was in part the result of a radical upsurge in the wake of the Great Depression. One of the most active political organizations in the United States at the time was the Communist Party (CP-USA) which began its work of labor organizing through the Trade Union Education League and later the Unemployed Council. The CP-USA, through its affiliation with the Third International, became very interested in the revolutionary movements in China, particularly the Chinese Communist Party, a sympathy shared by many members of the Anti-Imperialist Alliance. It was not surprising, then, that the CP-USA developed a close relationship with the alliance and also had a great deal of influence on certain elements in the Chinese left. For instance, the alliance's Union Square headquarters and the *Chinese Vanguard*'s office were originally in the same building as the CP-USA's own organ, the *Daily Worker*. The party provided the *Chinese Vanguard* with office space and printing facilities, and many news items appearing in the paper came from the *Daily Worker*.[5] The *Chinese Vanguard* was viewed as part of the party's program of outreach into New York's various ethnic and minority communities. An editorial in the party magazine, the *Communist*, even discussed the possibility of consolidating various foreign-language papers, including Greek, Ukranian, Italian, and Chinese, under its aegis.

One result of this connection was that the Chinese left became increasingly concerned with organizing workers in Chinatown. The alliance had moved to New York in part because there was a larger Chinese population to work with there, and its New York chapter was known as the Ssu Chao-jen Branch—Ssu being a Communist leader known for his efforts as a worker organizer, particularly in the famous Hong Kong–Canton Seamen's strike of 1922.

The Anti-Imperialist Alliance's first task was to rally the Chinese community to support its anti-Japanese position. The alliance pointed out that although Chiang Kai-shek had made a verbal commitment to resist the Japanese, in fact he was engaging in a civil war, and a truly united effort against the Japanese could not therefore come about as long as he was in power. This position was viewed as a partisan attack on the KMT, which accused the alliance of being "anti-Chinese" and banned the *Chinese Vanguard* from Chinatown newsstands. Anyone caught reading the paper, the KMT threatened, would be denounced to the Immigration Office as a Communist.[7]

The alliance's second task was to organize the workers in Chinatown, difficult in a community where work relationships were structured along clan and village lines. Attempts to organize along class lines confronted traditional values and challenged the power of the established associations, and most alliance members in any case had not had any previous experience with mass organizing and were not themselves well integrated into the daily life of the community. Many did not originally come from Chinatown, while others tended to avoid intimate social contact with people in the community.

In the light of these difficulties, the alliance decided to concentrate on raising the level of consciousness in the community. It tried to organize outdoor rallies, but such gatherings met with considerable opposition from the traditional associations and on several occasions alliance members were roughed up by local gangs. The focal point of its propaganda efforts, therefore, became the *Chinese Vanguard*. The paper began as a weekly, and attempted to provide its readers with a broad base of political knowledge as well as an awareness of the labor movement at home and abroad. The first page generally reported international news, with particular emphasis on Japanese moves against China and on political developments within China itself. The second page focused on strikes and other aspects of the labor movement. The third page kept readers informed of events in Chinatown and of the activities of the alliance, and feature articles appeared on the last page. The *Chinese Vanguard* did not pretend to be anything other than a political paper. Unlike other Chinatown periodicals, it did not carry crime or human-interest stories, serialized novels, or entertainment news. It did, however, help New York's Chinese—young people in particular—to become aware of conditions and developments outside their own community, exposing them to ideas that challenged traditional values.

The alliance's ultimate goal, of course, was to use the *Chinese Vanguard* not just for political propaganda and educational purposes but as an organizing tool. Since the KMT had banned the open sale of the paper, distribution had to be through individual contacts, and alliance members were urged to push the paper not only among friends and relatives but among workers in restaurants, laundries, groceries, on ships, and in factories and schools. The strategy was to contact potential working-class recruits in the process of selling the paper, and then to encourage the new members to make similar efforts to enlist their own friends, thus building a "network" of working-class contacts. The organization took this program seriously, even running a contest to see which group of cadre could sell the largest number of subscriptions.[8]

Despite these activities, the alliance did not make much headway. On February 15, 1933, the *Chinese Vanguard* published a self-critical article describing the concrete difficulties of organizing in Chinatown:

> Most Chinese in America, because of their ineligibility for naturalization and their lack of family life, do not intend to stay in this country for long. Many of them dream of making a small fortune and returning home. Understanding this mentality of the Chinese people, the feudal overseas establishments have tried to promote it further through the help of village and clan associations, shifting the attention of the Chinese masses to what is going on in China rather than here . . . thus diverting the masses' awareness of class conflicts, and preventing the development of class struggle here in Chinatown. As a result, the starting point of the masses' awareness is Chinese politics and not the class contradictions in Chinatown.

While recognizing these "objective" difficulties, the article also acknowledged specific problems in the alliance's own leadership:

> The Anti-Imperialist Alliance is a hard-core organization of all the politically conscious elements in the Chinese community. Its original members were left-wing elements in the KMT. They had been rank-and-file leaders of that party and were not from the Chinatown masses. Under the opportunistic leadership of the KMT, these leftist elements did not know or appreciate the problems and sufferings of the masses. Although they have worked hard in recent years to move closer to the masses, the bad influence of the old KMT days is difficult to get rid of in a short time.

This separation between the organization and the masses, the article went on, could be attributed primarily to errors of "elitism" and "dogmatism" committed by the cadres:

1. The Alliance cadres, with their overbearing abstract and theoretical concerns, ignore the concrete problems that face the masses:

Before we became politically conscious, we were just like the masses . . . unable to see the causes of our oppression and suffering. But after contact with other politically "advanced" elements, we came to realize that capitalism was the cause of our sufferings. Yet with this realization, we became preoccupied with the general aspects of capitalistic contradictions and forgot that the day-to-day problems faced by the masses are also part of the contradiction of capitalism. In fact, we paid no attention to their problems. If we could not even appreciate what the masses needed, how did we expect the masses to come to us?

2. The cadres look down on the masses and are not willing to educate them politically.

Our own political awakening was not God-given, it had to go through many stages. We had the good fortune of meeting politically "advanced" elements, or stumbling upon good revolutionary literature. Yet once we became politically conscious, we forgot the very processes we had gone through. Instead, we looked on them as enemies to the point of calling these working-class people "anti-revolutionary," "capitalists" . . . no wonder that the masses consider us political people as "crazies."

3. The cadres mouth slogans, and yet provide no concrete leadership for the people to follow.

We political elements could not bring about political change through stirring up spontaneous uprisings . . . careful plans and strategies had to be worked out. But new strategies are difficult to develop. Instead, we chose the easy way out by shouting revolutionary rhetoric and condemning the backwardness of the masses. [9]

This was harsh and frank self-criticism, reflecting the frustration of a highly political group at its inability to convert theory into practical work. In the past the alliance had relied too heavily on theories derived from other people's experiences, mainly those of the Chinese and U.S. left; now it had to develop a politics based on work in its own community. The first step was its attempt to organize Chinatown's unemployed.

THE CHINESE UNEMPLOYED COUNCIL

The Great Depression, which had begun in 1929, came to a
head in 1932–1933, and by the spring of 1933, 15 million people
were unemployed. As usual in a depression, minority-group and
foreign-born workers suffered the most, and the Chinese were no
exception. As unemployment rose, fewer people could afford to
use Chinese laundries, while those who could brought in fewer
items (no more underwear, socks, handkerchiefs, and sheets) and
less expensive work (common shirts rather than the high-collar stiff
variety). Some customers left clothes to be laundered, but didn't
have enough money to retrieve them. The restaurant business was
hit even harder. Many closed for lack of customers, while others had
to fire workers and cut prices drastically in order to survive. There
were regular reports of customers refusing to pay after eating.[10]

Many Chinese held to traditional concepts of pride and would
not lose face by admitting they needed help. Few Chinese were
ever seen on bread lines, and few applied for Federal Emergency
Unemployment Relief.* The unemployed rate in New York's
Chinatown was officially put at 30 percent, or between 6,000 and
7,000 people, but the figure was probably higher since much
unemployment was obscured by the mutual-aid functions of the
local associations. Some unemployed Chinese received temporary
room and board from their fongs; others were able to split full-time
jobs with fellow members.

While the traditional system served to alleviate the worst effects
of the depression for some, by late 1932 it was clear that others in
the community were not so fortunate. There were reports of
tenants being evicted for nonpayment of rent, of old men starving
to death in their apartments, of suicides committed after prolonged

---

*The Federal Emergency Relief Administration report shows that the percentage of
Chinese who sought relief was far lower than that of blacks and whites. In New York City,
the figures were: blacks, 23.9 percent; whites, 9.2 percent; Chinese, 1.2 percent. Even
today, some community leaders proudly recall that before 1933 no New York Chinese ever
asked for public assistance.

periods of unemployment.[11] Many Chinese left the country altogether, some migrating to South America.

In 1932, a group of unemployed Chinese, with the backing of the Chinese Anti-Imperialist Alliance, set up an Unemployed Council in Chinatown. This was not the first of such councils: the first had been established in 1930 and by 1931 there were nine in New York City alone. Across the nation, the councils, organized by the Communist Party, were a means for the unemployed to demand greater public and private relief, acquire emergency food supplies, and fight evictions.[12] Members of the alliance had been involved in the council movement even before the founding of the Chinatown branch.

On January 7, 1933, a notice of the establishment of the Chinese Unemployed Council was distributed in the community:

> Fellow workers, the present economic crisis is getting worse, our hardship of being unemployed is also becoming more difficult to bear, so many around us have no food, clothing or shelter. Can we possibly sit here and do nothing waiting for death to come? No, of course not. The only way out for us is to centralize all the strength of the unemployed. Therefore, the reason we want to form this organization is to solve the hardships and the sufferings of the unemployed. In one month of canvassing for support, we received an overwhelming response from the community. As a result we decided to go ahead with the formation of an unemployed organization on January 4th. In order to rally all the forces, we hope all fellow unemployed workers will participate in this movement actively. 7 Hester St.[13]

On January 13, the organization held its first membership meeting, which was well attended, reflecting the seriousness of the unemployment problem in the community. Several resolutions were passed:

> (1) The organization will be named the Chinese Unemployed Council–Greater New York; (2) the objective of the organization is to unite with all the forces of the unemployed, seeking assistance wherever possible; (3) all those who agree with the objectives of the

organization and help with the work can become members of the organization, regardless of whether they are employed or not, their political leanings, or clan or village distinctions; we also hope all associations and organizations will join us . . . (5) our present tasks: (a) to provide emergency aid to those without food and shelter; (b) to investigate the extent of the problem of unemployment in the community; (c) to unite with American unemployed movements, strengthening Chinese-American unity; (d) to request assistance from federal and municipal sources.[14]

The organization got right to work on its "present tasks," soliciting assistance from other New York unemployment groups to fight the illegal eviction of a Chinese tenant. It also appealed to local businesses to donate items for relief, and many people responded by sending clothing, rice, and newspapers. The Unemployed Council soon claimed a membership of several hundred; when it moved its headquarters into the center of Chinatown, it was a sign of growing self-confidence.

This was the first social-welfare organization in Chinatown that was independent of family, village, or district ties, and its success represented an embarrassment and challenge to the traditional associations. The mere fact that some Chinese went to the council for help was an acknowledgment of the failure of the old system. The traditional associations could not attack it directly, because it was addressing an issue of great concern to many in the community. Even the KMT, usually intolerant of any leftist working-class movement, took a neutral position toward the new organization.

The Chinese who joined the council must have realized that the socioeconomic system, not the individual, was responsible for unemployment. Moreover, the U.S. unemployed movement as a whole, organized by working people with leftist political leanings, had an antigovernment and anti-big-business orientation. The fact that some Chinese were willing to participate may be seen as an indication of a growing political radicalism, as well as of a desire to reach beyond the narrow confines of the Chinatown community.

At its second meeting, the council members decided to send

a delegation to the Chinatown Chinese Benevolent Association (CCBA) to ask for official endorsement and support for the council's efforts to aid the unemployed. The CCBA was reluctant to comply, yet to turn down such a "good-natured" request would clearly damage its public image. So it stalled for almost a month and then, when it did answer, refused to grant financial support: relief work, it said, should be carried out by family and district organizations, independently and voluntarily. In an editorial entitled "The Way to Resolve Unemployed Problems," one of the KMT papers not only agreed that "we should continue to follow the traditional way," but threatened that "all those Chinese who participate in political organizations may be in danger of 'being deported' by the Immigration Office."[15]

Such threats did nothing to enhance the CCBA's reputation, while the council, in contrast, appears to have emerged unscathed. Yet it was having internal problems of its own. Its leaders were becoming increasingly politically oriented, and preoccupied with the unemployed movement on a national level. Delegates were sent to a national unemployed demonstration in Washington, D.C., demanding better government policies for the unemployed, and it took a public position condemning "racial discrimination" in the government's policy of dispensing relief.[16] As the primary focus shifted away from the concrete work of helping local unemployed Chinese, many of the moderates left the organization. By 1934 it had only forty members.

The decline of the council was not, however, a purely local phenomenon but was part of a nationwide change in the strategy of the labor movement. With the passage of the National Industrial Recovery Act—part of which, Section 7a, granted organized labor the right to collective bargaining—there was a shift in emphasis away from the unemployed themselves to organizing industrial workers to fight for improved job security and higher wages.

But while the fate of the Chinese Unemployed Council was hardly unique, its demise underscored certain problems specific to the Chinese left. The formation of the council had originally been seen by the Chinese Anti-Imperialist Alliance as a way of addressing the day-to-day problems of the masses, and in this respect it was to a certain extent successful. Yet the unemployment issue managed to build only a temporary bridge between the alliance and the community. When the work of the council came to an end, there was no follow-up project, and without this the alliance's later attempt to establish a workers' center would prove unsuccessful.

If the Anti-Imperialist Alliance failed to speak to the great mass of Chinatown workers, this was in no small part due to its persistent elitism and dogmatism. Lack of experience was one problem, but graver still was its tendency to be overly influenced by other movements whose objectives were not necessarily appropriate to the Chinese community. It is true that the principal movements with which the Chinese left came into contact tended to be the most radical and highly political groups, for only those who had some appreciation of the racial discrimination and occupational exclusion suffered by the Chinese in this country would be interested in working with them at all. For instance, in the 1920s the anarchosyndicalist Industrial Workers of the World (IWW), believing that fraternal bonds existed among all wage earners, regardless of race, set about recruiting Asian workers into unions. Although the IWW was not wholly successful in this goal, it did attract a number of Chinese, and several groups and journals with anarchist leanings appeared in New York's Chinatown. Then in the 1930s the Communist Party made a considerable effort to reach out to workers in New York's Chinatown, in line with its strategy of trying to recruit the "most exploited," "most oppressed"— and therefore potentially the most militant—sectors of the working class. To the CP, the people of Chinatown were victims of racial oppression, but they were exploited workers as well, and as such offered a likely target for its organizing efforts.

However, the CP-USA's ideological positions only clouded the Chinese leftists' perceptions of their own situation. The Chinese were not in fact an integral part of the U.S. working class, and the most urgent task confronting them was to build a base within

Chinatown in opposition to the traditional associations. Yet the Anti-Imperialist Alliance continued to talk of uniting with fellow workers in waging a class struggle, without realizing that such theoretical abstractions only made them appear "dogmatic" to others. They attributed their repeated failures to what they disdainfully called the "low political consciousness" of Chinese workers and often preferred participating in political struggles outside of Chinatown. In fact, the Anti-Imperialist Alliance had a much better relationship with the U.S. left than with the community it was trying to organize. When the *Chinese Vanguard* celebrated its third anniversary, it was the CP-USA that organized a celebration at Manhattan's Lyceum Theater.[17] And when members of the alliance were persecuted by the Immigration Office for their political activities, it was the International Labor Defense, a left-wing legal organization, that came to their defense, saving many from deportation.

The CP-USA's interest in the social revolution going on inside China also offered many opportunities for joint activities with Chinese leftists. The party viewed the struggle for independence in China as a direct attack on imperialism, and as the realization of the Leninist strategy of an alliance between socialist forces and national bourgeoisie in semicolonial countries. It therefore paid close attention to events in China, with reports and analyses (by Earl Browder and other high-ranking party officials) appearing regularly in the *Daily Worker* and the *Communist*. Moreover, when Chiang Kai-shek destroyed the CCP-KMT coalition, attacking both Communists and labor activists, the CP-USA, joined by other sectors of the U.S. labor movement, openly expressed its outrage. In 1933, for instance, some eight hundred Americans and a few Chinese demonstrated in front of the Chinese consulate in New York to condemn the Nanking government's imprisonment of Huan Ping, a Chinese labor leader and chairman of the All-China Federation of Labor.

Although this sort of collaborative effort doubtless gave Chinese leftists valuable exposure to the workings of CP-USA and other such groups, it also tended to divert their energies away from developments within the Chinese community. The Chinese left was so busy working with the U.S. left that it failed to perceive an emergency situation right on its own doorstep: the plight of the most important Chinese occupation of all, the hand laundry business. And so, ironically, the movement that arose out of this crisis—a more than worthy successor to the Unemployed Council—was organized not by the Chinese left but by the laundrymen themselves.

THE CHINESE HAND LAUNDRY ALLIANCE

The hand laundry trade was hit hard by the Great Depression; there was sharp competition for whatever business remained, and the Chinese—as had happened so often in past economic crises—became the targets of increasing hostility. A series of incidents finally precipitated a crisis that threatened the very survival of all Chinese hand laundries in New York City, and the Chinese laundrymen, who had never before been political, organized in order to survive. In the process, they formed an association that was to remain the largest and most independent in Chinatown for years to come.

According to the 1920 U.S. Census, 30 percent of all Chinese were engaged in laundry work, and the figure was probably higher in New York City, where the Chinese were generally less well off and the number of people engaged in service trades consequently higher. During the 1930s there were 3,350 Chinese hand laundries in the city, and by 1940 37.5 percent of all Chinese were engaged in laundry work.[18]

The Chinese moved into this area not because of any "natural" aptitude for the trade, but because it required a minimum amount of capital (rent a room, and you were in business), little skill, and only a few words of English. Moreover, it offered independence—and thus none of the problems that invariably arose when working for or with non-Chinese. Laundry work was highly intensive (a ten-to-sixteen-hour day, six days a week, was common) as well as exceptionally tedious and monotonous; hence, the Chinese faced little competition from other laundries until World War I, when steam presses and washing machines were introduced.

Paradoxically, because they were self-employed (most owned their businesses, alone or in partnership), the Chinese laundrymen were not part of what is traditionally considered to be the working class. Yet in another sense they were the most menial workers. Although they might hire assistants to help out during a busy period, there was little division of labor within each laundry. Furthermore, such assistants usually came from the owner's clan or village, keeping class friction to a minimum and helping direct any antagonism toward competitors, Chinese and non-Chinese alike.

Although the laundrymen's immediate objective, not unnaturally, was to provide for their own survival and that of their families in China, their ultimate goal was often to return home and live in retirement as small landowners. "The life of the laundryman is not organized around his occupation here," sociologist Paul Siu observed. "It is organized around the possibility of the return trip, rather than the laundry itself."[19] The laundrymen, with their homeward orientation, "petty" property-owning aspirations, and lack of class consciousness, seemed to the Chinese left to offer little potential for political organizing.

Indeed, at this stage the laundrymen did lack a strong organization of their own. Most belonged to laundry guilds, which regulated competition by setting minimum prices and assigning a maximum number of laundries to each territory. And since a guild was generally subordinate to a tong or association, the laundrymen as a group were divided along clan, district, or family lines. The associations and tongs were more interested in extracting fees and dues from the laundries than in representing their interests.

The rapid developments in the U.S. laundry industry during the 1930s came as a severe shock to the Chinese. Large-scale non-Chinese laundries cut costs by introducing washing machines, steam presses (often operated by cheap black or immigrant female labor). The Chinese laundrymen, lacking the capital to modernize, had to attract customers by providing extra service—free mending, for example, or pick-up and delivery—and by keeping their prices one or two cents lower than those charged by the mechanized laundries. Evidently, these strategies were successful enough to be considered a serious threat. An article in one of the laundry trade journals complained that the Chinese laundrymen's policy of regular pick-ups at their customers' homes was taking a large volume of ironing work away from the mechanized laundries. They would continue to lose business, the article warned, as long as they continued to pick up "collar work" (ironing shirts) in a "hit and miss" fashion.[20]

As competition intensified, New York's non-Chinese laundries formed a citywide trade organization and requested the Chinese laundrymen to abide by the industrywide minimum prices it had established. When the Chinese refused, claiming they could not raise prices without losing customers, the trade organization retaliated with a massive boycott of the Chinese laundries. Once again, as in California during the late nineteenth century, the Chinese were made the scapegoats for all the ills of an economic depression. And, as before, this was a highly "racial" attack: a scurrilous cartoon poster appeared in store windows throughout the city, showing a Chinese laundryman with queue and buckteeth using his spit to wet the clothing before ironing. The poster campaign was effective and the Chinese laundry business began to suffer. Only when the Chinese consul-general enlisted the co-operation of the New York Police Department were storeowners convinced to take down the posters.

But this was only the first round of the attack. Early in 1933, New York's non-Chinese laundries convinced the Board of Aldermen to pass a laundry ordinance establishing a $25 yearly registration fee and requiring one-person laundries applying for a license to post a $1,000 bond, supposedly to cover the possible loss of customers' property. The bond (which represented a substantial outlay even for the larger, mechanized laundries) seemed specifically designed to drive the Chinese out of business, for there was no way a small "family"-run hand laundry (which averaged only $400 to $500 a year in profits) could raise that much money.

How were the laundrymen to stop this ruling, divided and unorganized as they were? Neither the CCBA, the nominal representative of the community, nor any of the other traditional associations showed any interest in fighting the new ordinance. The CCBA had become corrupt, in no small part by "exploiting" the laundrymen, whom it now refused to represent. Every one-person laundry had to pay the CCBA a yearly $4 registration fee ($8 for a two-person laundry), and all transactions relating to laundry ownership had to be certified as "legal," for a $5 fee. Since there were about 3,550 laundries, and since they changed hands as people returned to China and/or sold out to pay gambling debts, these payments provided the CCBA with a substantial yearly income. Yet the money was seldom used for the stated purpose of providing the laundries with protection and representation; instead, it often went to finance lucrative CCBA administrative positions. Candidates for CCBA posts found it well worth their while to buy the delegates' votes, and though the price of a single vote for president could run as high as $50, in office just reaping the laundry dues alone more than covered the costs of the election.[21]

The CCBA saw each opportunity for "community service" as a chance to reap new profits. During the poster campaign, for example, it demanded a $1 fee from each laundry to look into the matter. The laundrymen paid; the CCBA did nothing. By the time the issue of the city ordinance arose, some of the laundrymen had learned their lesson. Others, however, still tended toward a fatalistic acceptance of the CCBA's authority and urged it to take action on their behalf. On April 16, 1933, the CCBA called a mass meeting in a local school to consider ways of stopping the "bond" ordinance. Several hundred laundrymen attended. But when CCBA leaders began to speak, it was not of solutions but of money—a proposed $2 fee from each laundryman. Several members of the audience who spoke up in protest were cut off; one was carried out of the meeting by CCBA "goons." There was no discussion of specific ways of fighting the ordinance.

The meeting opened many eyes, and a few of the more active laundrymen decided to establish an independent laundry association. A declaration of intent was published in the local papers:

> Ever since China's isolation and self-sufficiency were destroyed by the European and American imperialists, the Chinese economy has been shaken to its very roots. . . . The harsh economic conditions suffered by the Chinese subsequently forced many of us to move overseas to earn a living. . . . Most of us had no capital to start a successful business. Thus we ended up selling our labor in the laundry trade. This trade became the mainstay of Chinese survival in the United States.
>
> There are almost 10,000 Chinese in New York City working in the laundry trade, yet we have no organization of our own. The ones that claim to represent us are in fact exploiting us. Today, when we face a most serious crisis, the "holy" CCBA really cannot represent us. All that it tries to do is to use this crisis to make more money. Therefore we must set up an organization that truly represents our own interests.[22]

All laundrymen were urged to assert their independence from the traditional structure, transcending village and kinship ties to unite in the new association. Political differences were downplayed too: even the KMT argued for the laundrymen's right not to be continually exploited and supported their effort to form an organization of their own.

On April 26 the first public meeting of the laundrymen was to be held at a Catholic church on Mott Street. The CCBA and the other traditional associations, recognizing the threat to their hegemony, tried to sabotage the meeting. They began by posting public notices around Chinatown:

> It has been known that a group of self-serving rotten elements hope to use this laundry crisis to make private gain by setting up another laundry association. . . . All Chinese laundrymen are hereby forewarned not to be fooled by these elements. If you ignore this advice, you should expect to suffer the consequences.[23]

Then, on the day of the meeting, the CCBA sent representatives to stand on street corners and urge people not to attend. These efforts were to no avail, however: several thousand people showed up, representing two thousand Chinese laundries throughout the city. At last they had realized that their problems could not be dealt with individually, that a united effort of all Chinese laundrymen was required. Under the slogan "Laundry Alliance for the Laundry-men," it was decided to form the Chinese Hand Laundry Alliance (CHLA), an organization to be set up along trade lines, thus avoiding family, clan, and geographic divisions.

The creators of the CHLA attempted to ensure that it would not reproduce the corrupt and autocratic structure of the traditional associations. Its leaders were to be democratically elected by the membership from among all the laundrymen. Greater New York was to be divided into three hundred districts (approximately ten laundries in each), and every district was to send one delegate to a representative body. There was to be a supervisory committee made up of fifteen of these delegates, including a president, a Chinese secretary, and an English secretary. The CHLA thus became the first democratic mass organization in the history of New York's Chinatown.

The CHLA, with the help of two lawyers, proceeded to challenge the proposed "bond" ordinance, arguing that it discriminated against small laundries. The Board of Aldermen agreed to modify the ordinance by reducing the registration fee from $25 to $10, and the bond to $100. The CHLA thus won its first battle, and the victory greatly boosted its popularity and prestige. Little more than a month after its formation, it claimed a membership of over 2,400.

The leadership emphasized repeatedly that the organization was not only to be independent of traditional controls, but was to be the standard bearer of new values and practices in the community. In its constitution, the CHLA promoted the principles of democracy, austerity, and scrupulous honesty; it also urged cooperation and mutual aid among its members: "Members shall love and cooperate with each other, shall not help the strong to rob the weak, or by any other means scheme against other members of the organization. Such actions will be punished."[24] And in fact, in order to prevent the image of corruption, wastefulness, and financial exploitation of the members, such "old-fashioned" Chinese diversions as gambling and eating were forbidden at CHLA headquarters, and the custom of giving gifts at New Year's or other traditional festivals was also discouraged.

The CHLA was very serious about its responsibilities. The $3 annual dues were to be used to handle business-related problems, particularly those involving contact with governmental authorities: protesting laundry codes, applying for yearly licenses, and dealing with the police, health, housing, and immigration authorities. Only the president received a salary; the other officers got nothing but a $.25 transportation fee, and the U.S. lawyers generally worked for almost nothing. When the CHLA raised funds over and above its dues, it used them to help the unemployed or the families of members who had died.

The growth of the CHLA not only drew members and financial resources away from the CCBA and the other traditional associations, but posed a major challenge to the established community structure. It began a confrontation between "old" and "new" that was to polarize the Chinese community for years to come. It is to the early phase of this struggle that we now turn.

3
OLD AGAINST NEW: POLITICAL AND ECONOMIC CONFLICTS, 1933-1940

The power of New York's traditional Chinese "establishment" had been contested before, but the Chinese Hand Laundry Association, with its large following and progressive political outlook, represented the greatest challenge yet. The traditional associations, realizing that the CHLA's continued success could ultimately spell their downfall, were determined to use every means at their disposal to destroy it.

The first step was to start rumors that the CHLA was the tool of opportunistic, untrustworthy elements. In response to this, the CHLA issued an open letter to the CCBA, responding that "our organization has pure and honorable objectives; our members are of excellent character. We have no hidden motives, and we hope your organization, the supreme organ of Chinatown, will give assistance to our organization so that we can accomplish our simple objectives."[1] Clearly, the CHLA's goal at this point was peaceful coexistence. It requested a meeting of the leaders of the two organizations to discuss their differences. At the meeting, CHLA leaders reiterated their nonantagonistic attitude toward the CCBA and the other traditional associations, and asked why the CCBA had discouraged its members from joining the CHLA. The CCBA representative claimed to have no hostile intentions toward the new organization but maintained that the majority of associations within the CCBA felt differently. The situation was left unresolved.

The attack on the CHLA was then renewed with a drive forbidding the laundrymen to hold dual membership in a traditional association and the CHLA. The On Leong tong, for example, ordered the resignation of any members who also belonged to the CHLA, even requiring them to publish an announcement of their withdrawal in the community papers:

> To whom it may concern:
> I am due to take a long journey. I am hereby severing my affiliation with the Chinese Hand Laundry Alliance. From here on I have nothing to do with the organization.[2]

Since absolute obedience was the very essence of such associations, many laundrymen did drop out of the CHLA, and seeing five or six notices of resignation in the papers each day had an overwhelmingly intimidating effect on the laundrymen. Fortunately for the CHLA, however, the On Leong tong's order came at a time when a "tong war" was brewing between it and the Hip Sing tong. When On Leong ordered its members to withdraw from the CHLA, Hip Sing did not follow suit, and this temporary preoccupation made it impossible for the tongs to mount a united effort against the CHLA. There were other, more indirect strategies of attack, however, and a major target was a pro-CHLA paper, *Chinese Journal*. This was the only Chinese paper in Chinatown without any community backing. Owned by a U.S. publisher, Barrows Mussey Company, it was a strictly commercial venture,[3] financially independent of local political forces, and could thus take a more "objective" position in its reporting. This, apparently, gave it considerable popular appeal, for it was by far the largest Chinese paper at that time, with a daily circulation of five thousand.

The editor, Y. K. Chu, was a reporter by profession and a respected intellectual with an excellent command of English. His politics were liberal; a KMT member in the 1920s, he was now, while not an adherent of the Chinese left, a stern critic of the KMT establishment. He was born into a large immigrant family from

Kwangtung province and had many relatives working in New York's hand laundry trade. As a result, he had an intimate knowledge of the problems facing Chinese laundrymen and was often asked to assist them. When the anti-Chinese posters went up, for example, Chu volunteered to convince store managers to take them down. After he became editor of the *Chinese Journal* in 1932 he made sure the paper gave extensive coverage to the issues and problems confronting the laundrymen—not the least of which, in his opinion, was the failure of the CCBA and the traditional associations to lend their support to the struggle. When the ordinance crisis occurred, Chu became actively involved in the formation of the CHLA, and was elected its temporary spokesman.

With its up-to-date reports of CHLA activities and constant exposés of CCBA malfeasance, the *Chinese Journal* soon became a vital organ of communication between CHLA organizers and the masses of laundrymen. Without its help, indeed, it is doubtful whether the CHLA could have maintained its mass base, or been so effective in mobilizing the laundrymen for quick action.

Not surprisingly, therefore, the CCBA and the traditional associations decided that the *Chinese Journal* had to be stopped. Not only was the paper "stirring up trouble" among the laundrymen, but its critical view of the traditional Chinatown power structure was undermining mass support for the old associations even among those outside the laundry trade. On June 23, 1933, the CCBA dispatched a number of "gangs" to picket the *Chinese Journal* office and demand that it stop criticizing the organization. Businesses were instructed to discontinue their ads in the paper, and newsstand operators were warned not to sell it. In fact, copies were confiscated from local newsstands, and one newspaper vendor was beaten in broad daylight for refusing to comply with the ban.

But such violent incidents served only to rouse the community's sympathy, and the CCBA and the associations soon realized that they would have to adopt different tactics in the battle against the CHLA. CCBA officials secretly approached the commissioner of the New York City License Bureau and tried to discredit the CHLA by identifying its organizers as untrustworthy individuals with illegal immigrant status.[4] This, the CCBA hoped, would go far toward undermining the CHLA's role as the legitimate representative of the Chinese laundrymen. And they were right. The commissioner responded promptly with a new ruling requiring all small-scale laundry operators to be fingerprinted before they could get a license to operate. Once again, this seemed a measure intended specifically for the Chinese, aimed at closing down all laundries whose operators lacked "proper" immigration status. The fingerprinting requirement itself was of such questionable legality that it had the look of harassment.

The CHLA quickly moved to challenge the commissioner's ruling in court. Meanwhile, the CCBA, hoping to regain its influence among the laundrymen, also stepped into the fray, hiring two "prominent" lawyers to look into the case and stressing repeatedly that it had "appropriate" plans to deal with the fingerprinting issue. But things did not go according to plan. The CCBA lawyers, unlike those retained by the CHLA, were eager to negotiate a settlement with the License Bureau; the "adventurous" methods used by the CHLA, the CCBA claimed, would only harden the bureau's position and make a settlement more difficult. Such divisions weakened the laundrymen's case, and the fingerprint ruling was allowed to stand. But during the courtroom proceedings, when the commissioner was called upon to justify his ruling, he was forced to reveal his secret discussions with the CCBA, thus dealing a severe blow to its image in Chinatown.

It should be emphasized that there was a great contrast in the way the old and the new—the CCBA and the CHLA—set about organizing their constituencies. Not only did each organization draw its strength from a different sector of the community, but the two did not even share the same conception of power. The CCBA and the other "establishment" associations tended to use their dominant position in the community to exact compliance from their members. They expected disputes to be dealt with via traditionally acceptable channels: through appeals and arbitration by the parties involved along hierarchical lines, or through negotiations between leaders of the disputing parties, with a CCBA representative as a third-party mediator. In any event, leaders should act like "gentlemen," with what a Chinese proverb calls "calm and peaceful intentions," and should settle problems without public confrontations in which all parties lose face. Any party unwilling to conform to these norms was dealt with harshly, through blackmail, boycott, and violence. When struggles reached this level, the rights and wrongs of the issue became far less important than clan, family, or tong interests, and ethical niceties were no longer observed—it was a common tactic, for instance, to write anonymous letters to the Immigration Office about the "illegal" status of one's opponents.[5]

The CHLA had never been a part of the "establishment," so its struggle against the associations had to be conducted on a different basis. The CHLA's strength depended on its ability to stir up public opinion on its behalf; it was thus more interested in open debate over political issues than in "private" negotiations among leaders of opposing organizations. This approach ran counter to all conventional conceptions of "correct" behavior, and was bound to rouse the ire of the traditional associations.

THE CHINESE HAND LAUNDRY ALLIANCE
AND THE CHINESE LEFT

The Chinese laundrymen's movement arose in response to a crisis in the trade. Neither initiated nor backed by any particular interest or faction, it was not—initially, at least—embroiled in community politics, and this was perhaps one reason why it attracted so many laundrymen. The CHLA's apparent lack of "politics" also seems to have led other groups to underestimate its potential. Its militancy and energy came as quite a shock not only to the traditional organizations but to the KMT and the left as well.

This "oversight" was particularly ironic in the case of the Chinese left, which, as was noted earlier, had been trying for some time, with limited success, to build a working-class movement in New York's Chinatown. Why, then, did it fail to play an active role in the organization of the laundrymen's movement? The chief problem seemed to be its analysis of the class structure in the Chinese community and its unyieldingly rigid approach to political organizing.

The Chinese left, including such organizations as the Chinese Anti-Imperialist Alliance, saw class oppression and exploitation only along the lines of a two-class struggle—capitalists versus workers. While this perspective might serve in a fully developed capitalist society, years of discrimination and exclusion had given Chinatown a highly distorted class structure. Few Chinese had become members of the industrial working class, and there were no large-scale Chinese-owned industries in Chinatown. Most businesses were small, service-oriented enterprises in which owners were often workers as well; they could rarely afford to hire extra help, but even when they did, the distinction between employer and employee was blurred by common kinship or village ties. Yet the Chinese left, determined to organize "workers," focused its efforts on those employed in laundries, restaurants, and groceries, not on the owners of such enterprises. Such workers, they believed, should see the owners as their enemies, as the exploiters of their labor. But the workers tended to identify with their bosses, and to see their *competitors* as the primary threat to their survival.

The left's mistaken approach becomes immediately apparent when we look at the way the CHLA was organized. Although the laundrymen could not be organized as "workers" in opposition to capitalist forces, they were nevertheless oppressed and exploited— by Chinatown's merchant elite. As we have seen, the economic crisis forced the Chinese laundries to confront the traditional associations, demanding "democracy" and "self-determination," their own autonomous organization, and the right to free speech. To this extent the laundrymen were a progressive force, for the main contradiction in New York's Chinatown at that time was not between workers and capitalists but between the popular forces and the traditional feudal associations.

Eventually, the left in Chinatown began to recognize the errors in its analysis, and articles in the spring of 1934 in the *Chinese Vanguard* began to appear calling for a reevaluation of its position with respect to the laundrymen. One writer observed that the "Chinese Hand Laundry Alliance is an organization consisting of small service businesses, and they can neither be considered as feudal or capitalistic in form." Another asserted that the "Chinese laundrymen are part of the 'laboring' class, and in their struggle against racially discriminatory legislation and feudal reactionary forces in Chinatown they are to be seen as allies of the proletariat."[6] The paper went on to give extensive coverage to the conflict between the CHLA and the CCBA, showing great sympathy and support for the former.

Before long, the Chinese left had undergone such a change of heart that it began to court the laundrymen, even suggesting an alliance with them. The CHLA was at first, wary of such overtures, but with the clamp-down imposed by the traditional associations, it could not expect open support from the general public, and the left became the only reliable ally in the community.

One of the first opportunities for joint action came in late 1933, when the CCBA and several large district associations initiated a slander suit against Chu, the editor of the *Chinese Journal*. Chu had accused the CCBA chairman of making a deal with the American Laundry Association in Jersey City, New Jersey, to undermine the formation of the CHLA's New Jersey branch. The CHLA viewed the suit as a clear threat to its own survival—an attempt to silence its most important ally and its membership's chief organ of communication. The laundrymen immediately came to Chu's defense, charging that the CCBA was using the courts to attack freedom of expression and assert its dictatorial control over the Chinese community.

Elitist associations like the CCBA had ruled Chinatown for

almost half a century; they had been challenged before, but never in the name of "democratic rights." Thus, the CHLA's initiative clearly signaled a new type of struggle, reflecting the penetration of external political values into the Chinese community. Though such democratic notions were still strange to most Chinese, those who had been exposed to "outside" political movements, many of them members of the Chinese left, became ardent exponents of the new values—and also, not surprisingly, the most active supporters of the CHLA.

Soon after the CCBA's suit against Chu was initiated, the Chinese left began to mobilize in his defense, with several organizations demanding that the CCBA drop the charges. As the case gained greater notoriety, it also became heavy with political overtones—not always to the defendant's advantage. The prosecuting attorney charged Chu with being a Communist, and when a representative of the CHLA took the stand as a defense witness, he was grilled about the political associations of the CHLA. At one point during the trial the judge even mentioned that he had received "secret reports" branding Chu a Communist. At times, not Chu but the entire Chinese left seemed to be on trial, and this "redbaiting" had its effect: after almost a year of deliberation, the judge found Chu guilty of slander and ordered him to cease all criticism of the CCBA for three years. To leftists in Chinatown, it was clear that Chu was the victim of a political vendetta. After his conviction, in fact, the Immigration Office even made an unsuccessful attempt to deport him; the *Chinese Vanguard* promptly responded with an editorial claiming that the CCBA, the court, and the Immigration Office had conspired to persecute Chu simply because he was an outspoken ally of the Chinese Hand Laundry Alliance.[7]

The U.S. left and labor movements had also shown great interest in the Chu case, and such journals as the *Daily Worker* and *China Today* had reported on the lawsuit and condemned the CCBA. Indeed, the Chinese left had helped the CHLA cultivate such outside progressive forces, and these contacts proved very useful to the laundrymen—their legal advisor, for example, was Julius L. Bezzo, a leftist lawyer.

Broadly speaking, the issues that most concerned the CHLA—racial discrimination and the tyranny of feudal forces in China-town—had great appeal for the larger U.S. radical movement. On the labor front, for example, a drive to organize industrial unions in factories—to "organize the unorganized"—was being launched, and to help out in the laundrymen's struggle seemed a logical extension of the left's commitment to organize unskilled and immigrant workers.

Undeniably, the CHLA needed the support and advice of such experienced people. First, there was the bitter conclusion of the Chu case. Then, in late 1934, the New York City License Bureau ruled that all laundry license holders show "proper" immigration status. Like the "bond" and "fingerprint" ordinances of the past, this measure seemed aimed exclusively at the Chinese. Not surprisingly, the CCBA's position, announced at a License Bureau hearing, was that "all the Chinese would abide by the ruling."[8]

Within the CHLA, there were different opinions on how to deal with the issue. Some favored a legal challenge, fearing that an overreaction would only antagonize the bureau. Other, more radical, elements felt it would do no good to contest the ruling in the courts; instead, they wanted to mobilize public opinion. Many sectors of the U.S. left and labor movements, including the *Daily Worker*, the International Workers' Order, and the Unemployed Council, did come out with public condemnations of the ruling, calling it "racist." The Friends of China Committee, a pro-U.S. Communist organization that was holding a "Hands-Off China" conference in New York at the time, was particularly supportive, issuing a protest to the License Bureau in the name of its 190,000 members.[9] Such Chinese groups as the Anti-Imperialist Alliance and the Anti-Japanese Patriotic Society also joined the public outcry. This strategy evidently had its effect, and in 1935 the bureau withdrew the ruling.

TRADITION FINDS AN ALLY IN THE KMT

The traditional associations' attack on the CHLA was motivated not only by the threat the organization posed to their own power base, but by their alliance with the KMT, arch-antagonist of Communists and labor movements. In the past, neither the CCBA nor the associations had formed links with a party in China, for the home country's unstable political situation and low international prestige made such ties unprofitable, even risky. The associations and the KMT were nevertheless natural allies. Politically, both tended to be elitist: the associations, including the CCBA, eager to maintain the hierarchical order in Chinatown, were suspicious of noninstitutionalized mass movements and of any new political thinking brought in from the "outside"; the KMT, too, mistrusted mass movements and preferred programs of "change" instituted from above.

From a purely pragmatic viewpoint, the two groups could also benefit each other. The KMT's prestige among overseas Chinese had declined since 1927, and it needed the help of these communities, particularly for financial reasons. Since it was unwilling and unable to mobilize popular support, it decided to throw its weight on the side of the traditional hierarchy. As for the associations, now that China was effectively unified under a single internationally recognized government dominated by the Nationalists, they had much to gain from a closer relationship with the KMT. They might win certain government concessions and favors, including the facilitation of the import and export trade and a reduction of red tape and taxes in business transactions. Furthermore, if the associations' authority were "sanctioned" by the "national" government, they could expect a much-needed enhancement of their prestige and legitimacy in the Chinatown community. Thus as the CHLA increasingly gained support from the left, the KMT abandoned any pretense of neutrality and came openly to the aid of the traditional associations. What had begun as a conflict over economic control became political as well, and the whole community soon became involved in the struggle between the KMT and the CHLA.

The KMT's strategy was to try to weaken the CHLA by encouraging dissension within its ranks. At first, the diverse membership of the CHLA was able to work together to confront the immediate crisis in the hand laundry industry, as well as the racial discrimination of the municipal authorities. But as the CHLA found itself repeatedly locking horns with the traditional elite, many of its members became fearful that it would become a "political" rather than a "trade" organization. Some of these dissidents were simply apolitical individuals who preferred not to take sides; others, however, as members both of traditional associations and the CHLA, were dismayed at the conflict of interest between the two. Then, too, the idea of a mass movement was foreign to many laundrymen, who shied away from any "militant" action, opting instead for an "orderly," legal approach. Such individuals wanted neither pitched battles with the traditional forces nor intimate collaboration with the left. The CHLA's sole function, they argued, should be the defense of Chinese in the laundry trade.

These cracks in the unity of the CHLA appeared at such an opportune moment—just when relations with the CCBA were at their most strained—that some of the CHLA's more militant members began to suspect that the dissidents were being manipulated by an outside agency. It was far from reassuring when a KMT paper published an open statement by CHLA dissidents expressing their misgivings about "certain" people within the CHLA. By March 1934, the conflict was so intense that a split appeared inevitable. Yet when a vote of confidence was taken to affirm the CHLA leadership, there proved to be only twelve hard-core dissidents, and they were easily expelled.[10]

These "outcasts" immediately formed a new group, the Chinese Hand Laundry Association. Although it claimed to be an independent trade organization, it seemed to be heavily reliant on the CCBA. In its founding declaration (announced, incidentally, from CCBA headquarters), it not only identified itself as an "anti-Communist" and genuinely trade-oriented organization but pledged to follow the "leadership and guidance" of the CCBA.[11] Yet, even after months of recruiting, it could claim only about one hundred members. In fact, since many of these purported members were not laundrymen at all, the real figure was probably closer to fifty.

In contrast, the expulsion of the dissidents only strengthened the CHLA. Its membership increased from 2,400 to 3,200 in 1934, perhaps because CCBA and KMT pressure no longer served to intimidate the laundrymen and prevent them from joining. Moreover, when the power elite, by its own actions, shattered any illusion of its "peaceful intentions," the CHLA became increasingly receptive to left-wing ideas and directions.

Initially, the conflict between old and new had involved only two parties within the Chinese community: the traditional elite and the CHLA. Then, as each side recruited "reinforcements," two opposing political blocs took shape: the traditional elite sought the support of the KMT and of conservative elements in U.S. politics, while the CHLA found allies in the Chinese and U.S. left movements. With the involvement of these "outside" forces, the confrontation became increasingly complex, fraught with political overtones: what had begun as a local battle began to spread far beyond the boundaries of Chinatown.

ORGANIZATIONAL REFORM AND CONSOLIDATION

By mid-1934, the CHLA had weathered repeated attempts to destroy it and was clearly in Chinatown to stay. Having proved itself to be an effective opposition to feudal and conservative organizations, it had attracted many leftist and progressive groups, and assumed the role of the leader and spokesman of all of them. The traditional associations, recognizing that their monolithic rule was a thing of the past, prepared to make changes. In May 1934, the newly elected CCBA chairman declared a campaign for internal reform, which it was hoped would revitalize the organization.

This did not mean, however, that the conflict was over. In 1936, the KMT again tried to cause a split within the CHLA. This time, a small group of self-proclaimed "anti-Communists" brought a suit against CHLA officials, accusing them of "undemocratic" election procedures. The case went to the New York State Supreme Court, where it dragged on for months; meanwhile, the instigators of the suit continually provoked confrontations, often violent ones, within the organization. In April 1937, the court declared the charges groundless, a verdict that only enhanced the CHLA's image inside and outside the community. The story was even picked up by the U.S press, where the CHLA was praised as the most modern and democratic organization in Chinatown. [12]

With such victories, and with the continuing support of the majority of the Chinese laundrymen, the CHLA's position in the community became ever more secure, and its impact on Chinatown ever more striking. Many venerable leisure-time traditions—gambling, regular banquets, gift giving to gain favors—were increasingly viewed as antiquated and corrupt, and new political and social activities arose in their place. Study groups were organized to discuss current events in China, while a flying club trained volunteer pilots for the anti-Japanese struggle. One of the most successful social clubs in Chinatown, the Quon Shar ("Mass Club"), was organized by CHLA members as a recreational center for laundrymen. With its sponsorship of trips, dances, lectures, and other social and educational programs, the Quon Shar provided an alternative to the kind of leisure-time activities offered by the traditional clubs. It was also a specific asset to the CHLA, for by enabling its activists to get acquainted in a social setting, it reinforced the organization's strength with a network of close personal relationships. Perhaps most important, however, was that the rise of such organizations as the Quon Shar helped many Chinese to forge a new identity—to break away from the confines of associations based on family, clan, village, and/or tong ties. The people of

Chinatown had long been prisoners of a "sojourner" mentality, passively accepting current difficulties, simply waiting for the day when they could afford to return home. Now they began to think in terms of a better life where they were, in the United States, and to believe in their ability to achieve it.

One manifestation of this new sense of self was an interest in the problems of Chinatown's youth. Many young people were immigrants who had come to the United States under the "slot" system; they had a bit more education than the older generation and tended to be more liberal in outlook. The traditional recreations enjoyed by their parents—gambling in clubhouses, going to church—did not seem healthy to them, yet they had few other options available. All this changed in the mid-1930s with the establishment of the Chinese Youth Patriotic Society (Chinese Youth Club, for short), an organization for eighteen to thirty-year-olds. Two hundred young people joined almost immediately, for the club was something new, and was independent of any political party, association, or tong. Although its stated purpose was to promote the anti-Japanese struggle through propaganda, fund raising, and public education, it actually did much more. It called for the elimination of passive and decadent behavior, encouraging participation in "healthy" recreation and socializing instead. It also struck a blow against age-old male-supremacist practices by admitting women. Even though most of its members worked a six-day week, the club was able to maintain an active program, including photography, drama, and singing groups, a Chinese literature class, and the publication of its own journal.[13]

The Youth Club did, briefly, have a competitor, for the KMT and the traditional associations felt so threatened by its existence that they established their own organization, the Three People's Principles Youth Corps. This club, however, was little more than a creature of the KMT—one of its chairmen was even a party official—and its activities seemed largely to consist of unsuccessful attempts to "red-bait" members of the Youth Club. It existed on paper for a few years and then dissolved.

The importance of the Youth Club cannot be underestimated, for it was an attempt by the newly organized progressives to ensure that their work for change would be carried on by the younger generation. Equally significant, the club's members, unlike many of Chinatown's older residents, clearly operated on the premise that they would eventually become a permanent part of U.S. society. They were not content to struggle in isolation or to remain an "ignored" minority. In outlining its "basic tasks," the Youth Club specifically committed itself to promoting "friendship between the Chinese and American people," adding that it would seek assistance from sympathetic U.S. groups in working to eliminate such racially discriminating legislation as the Exclusion Act.[14]

Indeed, the liberalized atmosphere in Chinatown encouraged many besides those in the Youth Club to reach out into U.S. society. Previous contacts with the U.S. left and labor movements had generally been limited to appeals for political assistance; now there began to be some interaction on the social level as well. A few Chinese joined the International Workers' Order (IWO), a co-operative health-insurance organization whose second and even more important role was to sponsor social and political functions where members of different ethnic groups could meet. These informal contacts did much to foster mutual understanding and political solidarity between the Chinese and other groups; in fact, there was so much interest in the organization that a Chinatown branch was formed—IWO Lodge No. 678, which at one time had more than eighty members.[15]

By the late 1930s, then, a great deal of progress had been made against the oppressive conditions in New York's Chinatown and the community's isolation from the rest of U.S. society. Nevertheless, Chinese workers continued to be excluded from the relatively en-lightened leadership of the labor movement of the 1930s. Ironically enough, one of the major obstacles to integration proved to be the Chinese Hand Laundry Alliance, which had become such a force for social change in Chinatown itself.

NEW UNIONS, OLD GUILD STRUCTURES

By the end of World War I, the United States had become the most industrialized nation in the world, yet only 14 percent of its work force of 25 million was organized into unions of any sort, and these were primarily craft unions. When management tried to break these labor organizations by using immigrant and/or minority workers, they retaliated with policies of racial exclusion that soon became firmly entrenched within the craft-union movement.

By the 1930s, however, the craft unions were in decline. Technological advances had increased the scale of U.S. industry while simplifying its production processes; what these new industrial giants required were large numbers of unskilled laborers directly hired by management, not skilled workers selected through the union apprenticeship system. And if this new labor force was to bargain effectively with management, its unions could not be limited to a particular trade or craft but had to be industrywide. The largest union at that time, the American Federation of Labor (AFL), was at first unwilling to abandon the exclusive craft-union concept; as a result, in 1935 a group split off from the AFL to form the Congress of Industrial Organizations (CIO), which became the foremost organ of the new "industrial" unions.

The industrial unions, if only for self-protection, had to be more egalitarian in their membership policies. Otherwise, those not included would scab, which would depress wage levels and working conditions for all workers. Therefore, the CIO broke with craft-union tradition not only in organizing the unskilled, but in adopting a nondiscriminatory racial policy. While the organization of minorities progressed at a slow and sometimes uneven rate, the 1930s did witness the inclusion of unskilled blacks in a number of unions, among them the United Mine Workers, the National Maritime Union, and the United Auto Workers.

The Chinese, unfortunately, had not made the same inroads into the U.S labor force as some of the other minorities. By the 1930s, most Chinese were so completely trapped in their "chosen" professions that new immigrants, guided by family or village ties, automatically settled into these trades. Few Chinese even bothered to look into other possibilities, particularly since the traditional occupations came equipped with an intricate and complex system of trade guilds to insure mutual protection from outside competition. But while these guilds may have been a necessary expedient in the late nineteenth century, by the 1930s they had become the main obstacle to the integration of Chinese workers into the U.S. labor force.

In the 1930s, two major guilds dominated the restaurant and laundry trades in New York's Chinatown: the Chinese Restaurant Association and the Chinese Hand Laundry Alliance. Both were typical of the trade-guild pattern: first, they included employers and employees; second, they had been established primarily to regulate competition within the industry, which they accomplished through price agreements and by restricting the number of businesses within a given geographic area; and third, they served as representatives to the world outside Chinatown, as trade blocks that would resist any external threat to their survival.

This Chinese-centered, employer-employee type of guild organization was very much at odds with the prevailing trends in U.S. industry as a whole. In fact, in the non-Chinese laundry and restaurant industries the line between employers and employees was growing sharper, and in the 1930s unions were formed in both trades. The highly mechanized U.S. laundry industry, for example, employed unskilled laborers, often black women, who had to work as many as seventy hours a week for wages of $15 or less. The Amalgamated Clothing Workers' Union began organizing these workers to fight for higher wages and better working conditions, and in 1937 some 15,000 laundry workers won a $.35 minimum hourly wage, an increase of about 10 percent, and a 44- to 48-hour week. [16]

This period of struggle between workers and management in the U.S. laundry industry put the Chinese laundrymen in an awkward and contradictory position. As we saw earlier, there was constant friction between the large-scale U.S. laundries and their small, service-oriented Chinese competitors. At the same time, the Chinese laundrymen had no particular affinity for the workers in the U.S. laundry industry; they considered unions a threat, since their very survival depended on keeping costs—and therefore, wages—as low as possible.

The Chinese laundrymen's failure to identify with the interests of the workers in this situation suggests a fundamental ignorance of class distinctions that can in part be traced back to traditional Chinese values. Society, according to this view, is divided among family, clan, village, and geographic lines. Class divisions are secondary, and where they do exist—as in the feudal relationship between master and apprentice—they are seen as nonantagonistic. Even a rudimentary awareness of class was unlikely to be inspired by the laundry or restaurant trades, where the skill level was so minimal that there could be no question of masters or apprentices. Moreover, while the U.S. capitalist system had created a definite distinction between owners and workers, the Chinese service trades did not usually differentiate between employer and employees. As Ivan Light so succinctly put it:

> [Since] the Chinese have traditionally preferred partnership to solo proprietorship, their firms used relatively little hired help. Instead, the workers were partners and, therefore, co-owners of the firm. Partners were invariably clan cousins. Moreover, when hired labor was required, the partners gave preference to fellow clansman. . . . This spirit of clannish fraternity gave a distinctly cooperative character to traditional Chinese-owned firms, and so tended to reduce employer-employee tensions.[17]

Thus, while the spirit of internal unity and lack of class consciousness was traditional among the Chinese, it was also practical: a response to their exclusion by the U.S. social and economic system, a way of closing ranks in order to survive. For most Chinese in the 1930s, class cooperation was an accepted reality. Owners and workers alike wanted nothing more than stable prices and minimum competition within each trade. And so, when the Roosevelt administration proposed the National Industrial Recovery

Act (NIRA) in 1933, the Chinese laundry and restaurant trades were quick to support it. Here at last, they thought, was a means by which business competition could be regulated in their favor.

THE NIRA AND NEW YORK'S CHINESE COMMUNITY

In 1933, the United States reached the depths of the Great Depression and civil and labor unrest were assuming threatening proportions. The NIRA, passed in June of that year, was the new Roosevelt administration's response to this situation. The basic intent of the NIRA was to bring about economic recovery through a program of labor and management cooperation with each side making appropriate concessions.

On the business side, the NIRA prescribed the organization of each industry under government supervision and the elimination of cutthroat competition through the enforcement of fair business practices and standards. The act also called for a relaxation of anti-trust laws, permitting businesses to fix prices and control production in order to halt deflationary trends. This, the government believed, would ultimately stabilize prices and avoid the violent competition and price-cutting "wars" that had characterized the early 1930s.

As for the workers, the NIRA hoped to increase their purchasing power by guaranteeing minimum wages and maximum working hours. But the heart of the act, as far as labor was concerned, was Section 7(a), which stipulated as a matter of solemn law that workers be allowed to bargain collectively through representatives of their own choosing.

Although the NIRA seemed on the surface to be a workable program, it soon faced difficulties. The business sector welcomed the opportunity to set protective price codes against competitors; the workers, on the other hand, complained that it was meaningless to set minimum wages unless prices were controlled as well. If the minimum wage went up, they argued, so would the prices set by businesses, thus keeping workers at the same substandard level. Thus, throughout 1933–1934, while business supported the NIRA in the expectation of labor peace, workers tried to use the program, specifically Section 7(a), to win higher wages through collective bargaining. Even at this stage, however, workers were increasingly viewing the NIRA not as a tool but as pro-business. As early as June 1933, the Laundry Workers Industrial Union led 1,000 workers in the Bronx in an anti-NIRA demonstration,[18] and by 1934 many strikes bore the character of struggles against the NIRA. Ultimately, opposition to the NIRA became so great that the program was legally challenged and the Supreme Court found the act unconstitutional.

While activist and progressive forces in the U.S. labor movement thus rejected the NIRA as pro-business, the Chinese community, particularly the laundry and restaurant trades, welcomed it. In August 1933, the New York Chinese Restaurant Association called a mass meeting to urge the active participation of all restaurants in the NIRA program. Five people were selected to oversee the establishment and implementation of a price and wage code in Chinatown, and a propaganda team was set up to promote community support. On September 13, 1933, at least fifty Chinese Restaurant Association members joined in a citywide pro-NIRA rally.

As for the Chinese Hand Laundry Alliance, 500 of its members participated in the same rally, indicating an unprecedented degree of involvement in U.S. politics. Furthermore, the CHLA sent its own president to represent the Chinese laundries on the citywide Board of Laundry Code. And because Chinese support for the NIRA was so active and so unusual, when sixteen different service trades called a mass meeting at Carnegie Hall, it was the CHLA delegate who was chosen to speak for the laundry trade as a whole. "We Chinese laundrymen are just as desirous and just as anxious to obtain a higher standard as any man," he said. "Our men will support wholeheartedly any movement that has as its aim the bringing about of decent and human standards of life in industry and otherwise."[19]

Why did the Chinese restaurant and laundry trades give the

NIRA such enthusiastic support, when 30,000 U.S. restaurant workers threatened to go on strike if the Roosevelt administration approved the price and wage codes proposed by management under NIRA regulations? Did the Chinese really intend to comply with all the NIRA programs? In fact, as it turned out, they did not. What the Chinese hoped to gain from the NIRA lay in the area of price agreements: if the entire industry, including the Chinese, observed a uniform code, price "wars" would end and Chinese businesses could look forward to decreasing pressure from their U.S. competitors. But there was to be no restructuring of wage levels in Chinatown, since the establishment of minimum wages and maximum hours would not have served the interests of the Chinese businesses. Nor would unions: not surprisingly the Chinese laundries and restaurants consistently resisted all attempts by outsiders to organize their workers.

ORGANIZING DRIVES IN CHINATOWN

The first attempt to organize Chinatown's workers was initiated by the Chinese left, which was greatly alarmed by the pro-NIRA stance of the restaurant and laundry trades. If Chinese workers were supporting the NIRA, the left believed, it was only because the owners had told them they had no choice—it was the law. The owners continued to pay wages far below the NIRA minimums, but workers who protested were immediately blacklisted in Chinatown. To the leftists, it seemed that the only answer was for Chinese workers to join national unions.

They had a great deal of difficulty convincing Chinese workers of this, however. At first they thought this was due to the workers' traditional lack of class consciousness; later they attributed it to the weakness of their own ties to the working class. In 1935, the Anti-Imperialist Alliance claimed to have recruited twenty restaurant workers into the Restaurant and Food Production Union, a branch of the Red International Labor Union, but these individuals turned out to be working neither in Chinatown nor in Chinese restaurants.[20] At that time, in fact, the only Chinese restaurant workers to join a U.S. union—the Cafeteria Employees Union—were employees at the New China, a large restaurant near City Hall, just outside of Chinatown. The New China's workers were both Chinese and non-Chinese, and its owner was a Chinese who in 1935 agreed to accept unionization.[21] All other attempts by national unions to organize Chinese restaurant workers were directed at the larger Chinese restaurants outside Chinatown. In 1938, a Brooklyn AFL local set up pickets outside several Chinese-owned restaurants in Brooklyn, demanding that they hire union workers. In at least one instance, they were joined by several Chinese who worked in non-Chinese-owned restaurants, so alarming the Chinese Restaurant Association that it sent representatives to negotiate with the union. An AFL local in Manhattan, meanwhile, had announced an ambitious drive to organize all restaurants, including those owned by Chinese. But without at least a few Chinese members who could work to recruit others, it found itself temporarily stymied.

Nevertheless, the AFL continued its organizing efforts and by late 1939 it had recruited some Chinese restaurant workers and established a Chinatown branch, the Chinese Restaurant Workers Federation. The federation's announced objectives were to "organize Chinese restaurant workers into an organization that will represent their interests," to "promote unity among the Chinese and American workers," to "eliminate mutual distrust between workers and employers," and to "struggle against American anti-Chinese attitudes."[22] The AFL leadership thought this beginning promising enough to grant the federation a formal charter; it was affiliated under Local 211 and launched a recruitment drive. The federation began with a "Letter to the Restaurant Workers," which condemned the harsh working conditions, long hours, and low wages in Chinese restaurants and called on workers to demand "a $5 minimum [daily] wage for a waiter (not including tips), 15 cents overtime pay, $1.25 per week raise for cooks, and a 60-hour week for all workers."[23] If management rejected these demands, the workers were urged to picket the restaurants.

This "outside" involvement in worker-management disputes made the Chinese Restaurant Association uneasy about its own public image. In a bid for unity, the association invited restaurant workers and community leaders to a meeting and assured them that management was no less interested than they were in improving the condition of the Chinese worker. The association also decided to change its name from the New York Chinese Restaurant Association to the New York Chinese Restaurant Workers and Merchants' Association. The emphasis of the "new" group was to "promote the friendly relationship between restaurant workers and management."[24]

As for the association's AFL "competition," Local 211 proved unable to win any sustained support from the Chinese restaurant workers. The few who joined soon dropped out, in part because those associated with the union were fired and blacklisted in restaurants throughout Chinatown. More important than the resistance from management, however, were the very methods the union used in its organizing drive.

The AFL set out to organize Chinatown as if it were establishing a business. Since it had no local contacts among the workers, it got a Chinese named Seto Chen to head the local. He was not a worker, and he had not had any previous contact with the Chinatown community, yet he secured a five-year contract that gave him the exclusive right to organize workers in Chinatown for the AFL. Several Chinese newspapers then revealed that certain opportunistic KMT functionaries, seeing the union as a potential source of personal profit and political control, had joined its staff. Management used this revelation as a weapon in its attack against the union, while the left in turn accused the KMT of trying to use the AFL as a tool to control Chinese workers.[25] The ensuing "scandal" totally discredited the local among workers in New York's Chinatown, and in 1942 AFL headquarters revoked its charter.

Although the AFL's own bungling was partly responsible for its inability to organize Chinatown in the 1930s, it was not the only national union to fail at the task. Part of the explanation, as we have suggested, may be found in the very nature of the Chinese laundry and restaurant business. They were small-scale operations, primarily because of a lack of capital. Most Chinese immigrants were poor, but even those who eventually made a profit from their labors saved their money to send home to relatives or to buy land in China for their retirement. They did not reinvest their earnings in their businesses: most Chinese restaurants spent little money on decor, while Chinese laundries invested in such new technology as the electric iron only when their failure to do so would have driven them out of business.

This unwillingness to invest in capital improvements meant that the Chinese service trades generally remained small, labor-intensive, relatively unprofitable, and locked into traditional guild-type relationships. Since no large-scale capitalistic system evolved in these trades, no strong class-conscious proletariat could develop either—and no modern labor unions could supplant the guilds. This in turn meant that the Chinese continued to be isolated from the wider U.S. labor force until more favorable public attitudes allowed them to hold jobs in areas other than the limited service trades. This was a change that began to occur in the 1940s; and it was closely associated with political developments in Chinatown and on the international front.

4
THE PATRIOTIC MOVEMENTS, 1904-1943

The overseas Chinese population had consistently shown extra-ordinary concern for the welfare of their homeland, and they contributed substantially, spiritually and financially, to appeals aimed at strengthening and uniting China. In the late nineteenth century, when Manchu rule was threatened from within and with-out, Chinese in the United States supported the "reform movement" led by K'ang Yu-wei, once a court official, and set up branches of the China Reform Association throughout the United States. These local associations established their own military schools and newspapers (among them New York's *Chinese Reform News*, founded in 1904) and engaged in various commercial ventures, including a bank worth almost $1 million.[1]

But the hopelessness of the reform cause soon became evident, and many younger Chinese began to respond to Dr. Sun Yat-sen's call for a "democratic revolution" to overthrow the Manchus. In 1894, Sun founded his first revolutionary organization, Hsing-chung Hui, not in China but in Hawaii. Sun toured the United States five times between 1896 and 1911 and raised thousands of dollars, primarily from younger working people, who were less likely to have sentimental attachments to imperial rule, and from members of the Chinatown tongs, especially the highly political Chih-kung tong. Sun also drew many able-minded leaders back to China to work for his cause. He had such great appreciation for the overseas Chinese that he called them the "mothers of the revolution."

The period following the 1911 Revolution, when the country was torn with the struggles among the warlords, was frustrating for patriotic Chinese in the United States, yet they continued to support efforts to bring about positive changes in China. In 1913, Yuan Shih-k'ai reinstituted an imperial government; at the same time, he sold out China's territorial interests to Japan, acceding to the infamous Twenty-One Demands in exchange for Japanese support for his regime. When Sun Yat-sen called for a second revolution to overthrow Yuan, the overseas Chinese again gave their generous support.

Although China was an ally of the Western democracies in World War I and should have been considered a victor at the Versailles conference, it was forced by the Great Powers—including the United States—to cede Shangtung province to Japan. Embittered by this betrayal, frustrated by the impotence of their leadership, and inspired by the example of the Russian Revolution, the Chinese people began to stir, and patriotic mass movements developed throughout the country. Beginning in 1919 with the intellectuals' May 4th Movement, this awakening later spread to other sectors of society, particularly the working classes, and anti-imperialist labor movements were organized. As before, the overseas Chinese played a major role in encouraging and sustaining these new movements.

Why did the Chinese in the United States become so caught up in this patriotic fervor? Perhaps the major reason was that they identified China's fortunes with their own. They attributed their mistreatment in this country to their home government's weakness in the international arena and believed they were discriminated against not out of some generalized antipathy toward racial minorities but specifically because they were Chinese. After all, they argued, the Japanese were "Asians" too, yet they were treated with greater respect because their government was powerful enough to protect their interests.

Indeed, in the early 1900s Japan had protested so strongly against the treatment of its nationals in California that a U.S.-Japanese war seemed a distinct possibility. In 1905, at the height of this crisis, the U.S. president was Theodore Roosevelt, by all accounts a confirmed racist whose mistrust of "Orientals" is well documented. ("Japan is a Oriental nation," he once said, "and the individual standard of truthfulness in Japan is low").[2] Yet in December 1905, Roosevelt resisted an attempt to exclude Japanese immigrants from this country as the Chinese had been:

> It is unwise to depart from the old American tradition and to discriminate . . . save on the ground of that man's fitness for citizenship. . . . We cannot afford to consider whether he is Catholic or Protestant . . . whether he is English or Irish . . . Frenchmen, or German, Japanese, Italian.

But in the next paragraph came an important qualification: "The entire Chinese coolie class . . . legitimately come under the head of undesirable immigrants to this country."[3] Roosevelt's seemingly inconsistent position begins to make sense only when we recall that Japan, by its stunning annihilation of two Russian fleets and the severe mauling it had given Russian armies in 1905, had recently established itself as a first-ranking world power. Thus, Roosevelt feared that any slight to the Japanese in this country could touch off an unnecessary confrontation, whereas the Chinese could be abused with impunity. "Had China been stronger," it was often remarked in New York's Chinatown, "we overseas would not be treated so badly in this country." In this sense, the Chinese's patriotism grew in direct proportion to their increasing frustration at the ill treatment they suffered in the United States.

It should be stressed that the patriotism of the overseas Chinese was equally tied up with the development of nationalistic sentiments in China. Traditionally, when China was still a self-sufficient agrarian economy, the people's primary loyalty had been to family and clan, and the concept of nationhood was weak. But the rapid development of science and technology, along with the rise of expansionist military powers like Japan, shattered the old Chinese political and economic institutions. In order to survive in this new and more hostile world, the Chinese were forced not only to modernize their country but to transcend their traditional parochialism and forge a common loyalty toward China as a nationalist entity. Chinese nationalism was thus a defensive strategy that grew out of the country's resistance to imperialism; the fight for national independence went hand in hand with the struggle for national unity.

The patriotic movements, then, were progressive in two senses. First, since the overseas Chinese assumed that they would win respect only when their country did, for them patriotism became an indirect means of fighting for equal rights in the United States—a fact often missed by outside observers, who assumed the Chinese were a strictly apolitical, homeward-looking people. The second progressive feature was the concept of a united China, which would inevitably mean the breakdown of clan, family, and regional divisions. This posed a challenge to the very existence of the traditional associations in New York's Chinatown, and complicated the internal struggles there.

THE DYNAMICS OF THE PATRIOTIC MOVEMENTS

The overseas Chinese generally lent their support to any group they felt was fighting for China; they did not take sides in the conflicts among the various nationalist factions, and no single movement or party could claim their absolute loyalty. Objective results were the criteria of their support, and if they thought some party was not working in the best interests of China, they would turn against it—even if that party was the ruling KMT. In short, while their support for Chinese independence and social change was absolute, their loyalty to particular parties or groupings was conditional. It was for this reason that the leadership of the patriotic movements in New York's Chinatown was constantly shifting.

Prior to the mid-1920s, the only patriotic groups in New York's Chinatown—such as the Pao-huang Hui (Reform Association), led by K'ang Yu-wei, or the Tung-meng Hui, formed by Sun Yat-sen to rally overseas support—were aimed at the community elites, the leaders of the traditional associations and tongs, and operated through their hierarchical structure. As the patriotic movements grew, however, they became more mass-oriented and developed new, "national" loyalties that inevitably conflicted with the interests of the traditional associations.

In 1923, the newly reorganized KMT (see chapter 2) began to coordinate the patriotic movements on a mass level. When it called for a "united front" against imperialism and warlordism, New York Chinese from all walks of life and political factions joined the cause. The KMT grew stronger, building up such a significant mass base for patriotic activities that even the traditional organizations had to go along with it or else risk isolation from the community.

When China's growth as a nation brought a reaction from Japanese militarists, who had their own designs on the country, patriotic sentiments among New York's Chinese were again aroused. Following the Northern Expedition of 1927, which crushed the warlords and unified China under KMT leadership, Japan decided to intervene. On May 3, 1928, under the guise of protecting Japanese nationals, troops were sent to the city of Tsinan, where they massacred nearly four thousand Chinese civilians and destroyed countless businesses and private homes. In New York's Chinatown, the public was outraged, and when the local KMT leadership called for an organized response, a coalition of anti-Japanese groups, called the Chinese Citizens' Patriotic League of New York, was quickly formed.

The Patriotic League's first mass meeting, held in a local theater on May 28, 1928, was attended by almost five thousand Chinese. Its next action, an outdoor demonstration, attracted over ten thousand, representing 148 different organizations and groups (associations, restaurants, churches, stores, local schools, and social clubs). This show of solidarity with Chinese in China was aimed not only at the local community but at a broader public as well; the demonstration was followed by a procession through neighborhoods outside Chinatown, with participants carrying placards written in English. The Patriotic League sent cables to President Coolidge urging him to take a stand against the Japanese aggression as a threat to world peace. It also raised funds, collecting a total of $70,000 from the Chinese community in only five months. [4]

The successes of the KMT-inspired Patriotic League clearly revealed the effectiveness of the newly reorganized party. It was able to articulate patriotic sentiment that had long been present among overseas Chinese, and it was able to mobilize the whole community for mass action. Even the CCBA and the traditional associations took part, making their facilities available to the Patriotic League. Although they had never shown the slightest interest in patriotic movements, to remain indifferent now would mean popular condemnation. At the same time, the KMT's patriotic leadership in Chinatown, as well as its role as "unifier" and ruling party of China, forced the traditional associations to recognize it as part of the elite.

Unfortunately, by late 1928 the KMT *was* looking more and more like an elite. Now under Chiang Kai-shek, the party discontinued its domestic "united front," moved away from mass organizing, and concentrated on the liquidation of internal opposition, particularly the Chinese Communists. Until China was internally "united," Chiang claimed, it was in no position to offer effective resistance to Japanese aggression.

Following Chiang's lead, overseas branches of the KMT were suddenly forced to retreat from mass organizing, particularly around the anti-Japanese question. Many activists withdrew from the party or formed their own groups. By 1929, the New York KMT was in disarray, its popular appeal gone, and the community was left without an organization to mobilize its patriotic sentiments. The only group that consistently called for resistance against Japan was the Chinese Anti-Imperialist Alliance, which, as we have seen, did not have mass support in Chinatown. Furthermore, the alliance argued that the anti-Japanese struggle was only possible if the "traitor" Chiang was eliminated, and its slogan was "Resist Japan and Defeat Chiang." Most of New York's Chinese were not ready to embrace such an "extreme" position; they wanted a united effort of all Chinese against Japanese aggression, and factional differences made little difference to them.

Even with this lack of leadership, patriotic feeling within the community ran so high that on several occasions there were spontaneous expressions of concern for the future of China. In 1931, after the Japanese invasion of Manchuria, Chiang's government instructed local military generals to adopt a policy of non-resistance. General Ma, an officer stationed in Heilungkiang, disobeyed the directive and led his troops against the advancing Japanese, preventing them, for a time, from taking over the area. New York's Chinese were so elated by General Ma's heroic struggle that they set up an ad hoc committee to raise funds to send back through nongovernment channels. The news of General Ma's resistance was blacked out by most of the official KMT papers and by other papers closely linked to the party in order not to offend the Nationalist government. The only paper in Chinatown to give the story full coverage was the privately owned *Chinese Journal*, and it had to expand its daily circulation by 50 percent (from 4,000 to 6,000) to meet the demand; the paper's weekend edition was increased to 10,500.[5]

In early 1932, a similar act of resistance again stirred the overseas Chinese. When the 19th Route Army, stationed in Shanghai, was ordered to withdraw to avoid conflict with the Japanese military, some of the commanders refused to abandon Chinese territory. On January 28, Japan attacked with a force almost four times the strength of the Chinese, and for more than a month the defending troops held on under heavy bombardment from air and sea. Almost daily, individuals and groups in New York's Chinatown cabled messages of support to the Chinese troops in Shanghai. Although the local KMT and the Nationalist-run consulate were not enthusiastic, the Chinese community insisted on raising funds to send to the troops. Some money was dispatched directly to the Shanghai military command, some to the Nationalist government in Nanking; a few people even asked relatives in Kwangtung province to send their contributions on to Shanghai. Despite the high risk of funds falling into the wrong hands and never reaching the 19th Route Army, the Chinese abroad were determined to find a way to show solidarity with the defenders of Shanghai. The Nanking government, unfortunately, was not so supportive, not only failing to send reinforcements to the encircled troops, but even trying to use the outpouring of overseas support as justification for an 80 percent cutback in its normal supplies to the troops.[6]

After the Shanghai incident, the patriotic movement reached a low point, and there was a growing feeling that ineffective leadership was destroying the Chinese nation. The Nanking government began to use force against those who called for resistance to the Japanese, and many patriotic leaders were jailed. In New York, participants in anti-Japanese activities were branded "Communists" and "antigovernment traitors"; in some cases the KMT used the traditional associations to help intimidate dissenters, and this tactic was particularly successful.

Yet the patriotism of the overseas Chinese was so pervasive that it cut across family, clan, village, and party divisions; though it might be forced into temporary confusion or retreat, it could never be eliminated.

THE CHINESE WOMEN'S PATRIOTIC ASSOCIATION

Even during the dark years of the early 1930s, individuals and small scattered groups persisted in patriotic activities. The most significant and successful of these was the Chinese Women's

Patriotic Association, founded in the aftermath of the invasion of Manchuria. Women formed a very distinct grouping within Chinatown: as a result of the Exclusion Act and the immigration rulings of 1924, very few had entered the United States at all, and those who did were the wives of merchants. So the association's members, most of whom were married and had children, were liable to have different concerns from the single men who made up the majority of the community. Their families were not in China, so they were apt to identify with the United States—to be more sensitive to its political climate and to pay more attention to the long-range interests of the Chinese in this country. Thus, while the association's main objective, as stated in its founding declaration, was to "promote Chinese unity against Japanese aggression in China" through "fund raising and charity," it tended to interpret its patriotic activities broadly. It viewed the anti-Japanese struggle in relation to U.S. interests, calling for "propaganda against the U.S. isolationists" in order to prevent fascism from becoming a worldwide danger. It also declared that it intended to deal with "Chinese-American problems" and demanded "racial equality,"[7] apparently seeing no inconsistency between these issues and its patriotic concerns. Indeed, as we have already suggested, the desire to improve conditions for Chinese in this country was often a crucial motivation for patriotic activity.

Between 1933 and 1943, the Chinese Women's Patriotic Association used its high visibility to engage in a variety of successful fund-raising activities, including auctions, bazaars, charity balls, and the sale of goods donated by local merchants. As the only all-woman organization, it had an exceptionally stable constituency and was able to address its concerns clearly and forcefully. For many years, it joined left-wing groups in criticizing KMT inaction, and when the patriotic General Tsai Ting-kai, leader of the 19th Route Army, came to New York in 1934, it sponsored a welcoming banquet. In fact, it was General Tsai's visit that rekindled the patriotic mass movement in Chinatown.

A PATRIOTIC HERO COMES TO CHINATOWN

In 1934, as Japanese troops were threatening to cross the Great Wall of China, Chiang continued his policy of nonresistance and appeasement. Instead of fighting Japan, he mobilized 700,000 troops for the "Fifth Bandit Suppression Campaign" against the elusive and stubborn Communists, and criticism began to surface, even among moderates within the KMT. Fear of reprisals had long kept many dissidents silent; now national figures, including Madame Sun Yat-sen, called for the immediate cessation of internal conflict in order to unite all forces, including the Communists, against the Japanese.

General Tsai was one of the leaders who supported Madame Sun's call for national unity. Even though he had been demoted by Chiang for insubordination, he remained a national hero, a symbol of patriotic resistance to Chinese the world over. In 1934, he resigned his commission and embarked on an international tour to gain support for a unified Chinese resistance to Japan.

Tsai came to the United States to express his personal appreciation to the overseas Chinese for their support during the defense of Shanghai. At the pier in New York, he was greeted enthusiastically by some three thousand Chinese, and when his motorcade arrived in Chinatown, the community crowded into the narrow streets to cheer him. Such a welcome could only be interpreted by the local KMT as a clear indication of dissatisfaction with the policies of Chiang and the Nanking government.

The party was so alarmed that it tried various ploys to sabotage the visit. The Nanking government sent a field commander as its "official" representative, hoping to upstage General Tsai. And when the Chinese Hand Laundry Alliance organized a welcoming banquet at the New Yorker Hotel, KMT members tried to discourage people from attending by spreading rumors that the CHLA was full of "Communists."[8] None of these tactics kept the people away, however, and in the face of Tsai's overwhelming popularity, even some of the traditional associations turned out to welcome him.

The immediate task, Tsai told the Chinese community, was to unite all forces in China to resist Japanese aggression; civil conflicts must cease. At a press conference in New York, the general made the following statement:

> In my present journey to America, I have experienced the most heartfelt welcome from my fellow Chinese overseas residents, and I am most grateful. I have consistently advocated that China stand up and save our country by fighting against the Japanese aggressors. However, the authorities in power are willing to appease the Japanese and sell out our country. People like ourselves cannot accept decisions which violate our determination to have a powerful and united China, and must stand up and oppose such policies. The people's revolutionary movement has suffered defeats, but we are not disheartened. We still see a loyal defense for the survival of our nation as our god-given task. No matter what, if we are resolved to fight, I will be willing to pick up a gun and move at the head of the march. But more importantly, China is a nation of 400 million people, and resisting the Japanese is the uniform demand of all 400 million. If we fight and lose, all of us will be willing to accept the outcome. But we will never allow a few warlords and dictators to control the future of China and give up our sacred territories to our enemy. [9]

At every opportunity, Tsai called for a large-scale united movement. On the eve of his departure, he sent a farewell message to a local newspaper urging the overseas Chinese to "resolutely continue your fight against Japanese aggression, so the next time we meet we will all be in the same fighting front."[10] Tsai's visit clarified the direction patriots in New York's Chinatown would take: all differences were to be put aside and a united front formed to resist Japanese aggression; any who refused to join would be isolated and viewed as traitors.

THE FORMATION OF A UNITED FRONT

The Chinese certainly did not lack enthusiasm for a united movement; rather, what was missing was a leadership that could weld this energy into an effective force. Such direction could not come from the traditional elite, which saw the patriotic movement as a threat to its own political base, or from the KMT, which had to support official policy. A new organization was needed, and thus it is not surprising that the growth of the patriotic movement coincided with the rise of the political and labor movements discussed in the last chapter.

The Anti-Imperialist Alliance, for example, established in opposition to Chiang's nonresistance policy, attempted to build the patriotic movement by attacking and exposing the incompetence of the KMT leadership. As a result, the alliance was often perceived as no less sectarian than the KMT, guilty of letting internal squabbles take precedence over the task of national survival. Even in its partisan way, however, the Anti-Imperialist Alliance was truly concerned with the threat of Japanese aggression and did its best to inform the community of the urgency of the situation. Its paper, the *Chinese Vanguard*, provided thorough and up-to-date reports on the Japanese presence in China, and it distributed leaflets, set up rallies on streetcorners, and tried to organize forums and discussion groups to arouse popular interest.

The Chinese left's problems, however, went beyond its "partisan" image in the community. It lacked awareness of the masses' potential patriotism and, as in its organizing of the labor movement in Chinatown, focused only on the working people. In its view, the whole traditional power structure in Chinatown was opposed to the patriotic movement, and thus it attacked all family, district, and clan distinctions as unpatriotic. It was suspicious of nationalistic sentiments expressed by the petty bourgeoisie, which it considered as untrustworthy as the KMT, and the *Chinese Vanguard* even at one time branded General Tsai a warlord who had ulterior motives.

With this kind of narrow "class" perspective, it is not surprising the Chinese left had little success in building a patriotic movement.

After the invasion of Manchuria in September 1931, most national leaders in China, as well as the Chinese Communist Party (CCP), recognized that there was overwhelming popular opposition to the Japanese. The question was how it could be mobilized most effectively. The CCP's answer was a "united front from below," encompassing workers and peasants but excluding the petty bourgeoisie, national bourgeoisie, and other so-called "neutral" elements. The working people, under CCP leadership, would be organized to defeat the Japanese and at the same time eliminate the KMT and its bourgeois allies. Typically, the CCP gave no support either to opposition factions within the KMT or to those military leaders who disagreed with Chiang's nonresistance policy. To the party, the anti-imperialist struggle could not be separated from the domestic class conflict, and the overthrow of the KMT was a prerequisite for the struggle against Japan. As Mao Tse-tung put it in 1934, "In order to carry out the anti-imperialist campaign, we must unify all the powers to fight against the KMT, because the KMT is the largest obstacle that prevents an anti-imperialist movement by the Soviet government and the Chinese masses."[11]

In 1935, however, the CCP was forced to retreat to the hinterlands of China—the famous Long March—and its forces were weakened and isolated. A change in policy began to evolve as the party admitted the error of its "leftism" and "closed-door sectarianism" toward other anti-imperialist and progressive forces. In August 1935, the Central Committee issued an open letter to the KMT calling for the creation of a united front with the Nationalists against the Japanese and expressing a desire to cooperate with them in forming a democratic Chinese republic. This shift was the result of at least three factors: first, the majority of the people were eager to fight the Japanese and wanted no part of a civil war; second, moderate, liberal, and even conservative leaders recognized the need for united action against the Japanese and were being pressured by the people to unite with the CCP; and finally, the diehard anti-Communists represented such a small faction that they could be isolated. By renouncing its feud with the KMT, the CCP united its goals with those of the masses and was able to assume the leadership of the Chinese patriotic movement.

The formation of a parallel united front in New York's Chinatown was preceded by a similar period of changing strategies and shifting alliances. As we have seen, such leftist elements as the Chinese Anti-Imperialist Alliance had proved incapable of uniting the various patriotic groups, and this role was subsequently taken on by the Chinese Hand Laundry Alliance. Almost from its inception, the CHLA had taken an interest in patriotic activities, and while it was at first mainly one of many groups participating in rallies and discussion forums, it soon emerged as a leader. This had a certain logic, since it was the largest mass-based organization in Chinatown and had been founded because of the ineffectual leadership of the traditional associations and tongs; in forming an anti-Japanese movement, it was responding in much the same way to the inaction of the KMT and its allies.

The CHLA first joined with leftist organizations, such as the Chinese Anti-Imperialist Alliance and the Unemployed Council, in demanding the immediate formation of an anti-Japanese and anti-Chiang united front in the Chinatown community. To the left, the anti-Chiang stand was primary, since it was he and his followers who were preventing the Chinese people from forming a front against Japan. The CHLA, on the other hand, felt, as General Tsai had said, that the majority of the Chinese people were in favor of resisting Japan, while only a very small minority opposed it. It was not therefore necessary to tie the patriotic movement strictly to the class struggle, and if all those who agreed with the need for immediate resistance could be united, it would then be possible to isolate Chiang and his followers.

As soon as this modified position was understood, many liberal and moderate groups joined the struggle. In June 1935, the CHLA organized a "Resist Japan, Smash Chiang" forum which drew large numbers of individuals and community groups. By September, plans for a united Chinatown anti-Japanese organization had already been made at a meeting attended by the CHLA, the Chinese Anti-Imperialist Alliance, the Unemployed Council, the Chinese Women's Patriotic Association, the New York Chinese Student Association, the *Chinese Journal*, the *Chinese Vanguard*, and several small village associations. Although the participants would welcome any individual or group that supported their cause, they resolved to pay particular attention to "workers, women, students, members of the local press, and even members of tongs."[12]

The resulting New York United Anti-Japanese Association included most of the left and liberal groups in the community. Riding on a wave of mass enthusiasm, its membership was even open to members of conservative associations—it was felt that welcoming them would either cause splits in the conservative organizations or force them, under pressure from their members, to join the association themselves. The strategy was thus to not confront the traditional organizations head on, but to begin with their weakest link, the tongs, the least "established" and most independent of all the older community groups.

The Chih-kung tong (Triad Society, or Chinese Free Masons), the oldest and most political of the tongs, had a long history of activism in patriotic movements (it had been founded in the struggle to reinstate the Ming Dynasty in the seventeenth century) and was thus a likely candidate for recruitment to the new United Association, which played on this patriotic tradition. In one of several open letters to the editors of Triad's official organ, *Kun Pao*, the United Association noted that the tong had been founded for the express purpose of fighting foreign domination of China and had been one of the first groups to express open admiration for General Tsai and for his opposition to Chiang's nonresistance policy. Aware that Triad's reluctance to join stemmed mainly from its strong distrust of Communism, the United Association responded that the anti-Japanese campaign was more important than parties or factions. The primary opposition, it argued, should be to the "traitors" who were selling out China, and in a later letter it even urged support for elements within the KMT who were opposed to Japan and to Chiang.

After a few months of private discussion and open debate, Triad agreed to become part of the United Association, while making it clear that it still had reservations about the Communists.[13] With this new addition, the association made a giant step forward, and a "bandwagon" effect began. The On Leong tong, the largest in Chinatown, which was under the leadership of Seto May-tong, a shrewd and patriotic individual, declared itself opposed to "national traitors" and ready to join.[14] Leaders in the other traditional associations quickly realized that unless they agreed to participate, they would lose control over their own organizations. The CCBA held out for a while, but its members were repeatedly attacked as "traitors" and "running dogs" for the KMT government and on December 28, 1935, it called a meeting to discuss communitywide actions. On January 4, 1936, a new united front organization, the All-Chinatown Anti-Japanese Patriotic Association, was formed.[15] An executive committee of twenty included representatives from most of the local organizations and associations, right, left, and center. Similar patriotic associations were soon formed in all the major Chinese communities in the United States, and in each case political and organizational differences were set aside in the interests of national survival.

By this time, the only group that had not joined the association in New York was the KMT. It was completely isolated, and became even more so when it tried to "redbait" the new organization. Community criticism became increasingly open and direct. In August 1936, when the Chinese Communist Party sent an open letter to the KMT calling for the cessation of domestic conflict and unification to fight the Japanese, the CCBA signaled its agreement by cabling the Nanking government that "the whole overseas community is in opposition to the continued, careless pursuit of civil war."[16]

The KMT's growing isolation in the overseas communities was paralleled in China by increasingly violent internal opposition to Chiang and his policies. Finally, in December 1936, Chiang was kidnapped by General Chang Hsueh-liang, commander of the Northeastern Army and a staunch opponent of Chiang's "Sixth Bandit Suppression Campaign" against the Communists. Unless Chiang declared war on Japan, the general warned, he would be executed. In a mediated settlement involving several parties, including the Communists, Chiang was forced to agree to the cessation of the civil war and the formation of a national united front. The Chinese Communist Party, in turn, agreed to incorporate the Red Army into the national army of the central government, dissolve its soviet government, suspend its policy of struggle, and cease all propaganda against the KMT. All forces in China were thus nominally brought under the leadership of the central government and Chiang Kai-shek; a national united front against Japanese aggression was finally achieved. The Communists and the Nationalists, who each controlled different sections of the countryside, would continue to operate independently, but agreed to cooperate.

This dramatic turn of events put an end to KMT isolation in New York's Chinatown. At the same time, it enabled the left to become more active—for the first time, for instance, an overseas branch of the Chinese Communist Party worked openly without fear of persecution. Further, this spirit of unity was not limited to the two major political parties: all factions and groups agreed to work together, or at least to tolerate one another. As an editorial in one student journal expressed it, "We must confess that, before recent developments, we, the overseas Chinese, had the greatest difficulties in working together, but now in time of national crisis and in response to the uniform demand of all the overseas Chinese, we cannot help but work hard together."[17]

And it was none too soon, for on July 7, 1937, Japanese troops stationed at Lu-kou ch'iao on the outskirts of Peking fired on Chinese soldiers, precipitating the Sino-Japanese War. China moved into a nationwide mobilization.

THE SINO-JAPANESE WAR

Chinatown's dramatic response to the outbreak of the war was described in an article written several years later:

> As soon as the Lu-kuo ch'iao Incident occurred on July 7, 1937, the anger and frustration that had been building up for decades in the hearts of the Chinese people finally exploded. From that point the whole country, from top to bottom, across all parties and classes, united as brothers. This spirit of fighting external aggression head-on immediately affected the overseas Chinese communities as well. Once we heard that the first gun shot had been fired, initiating the Sino-Japanese War, we were able to mobilize the whole Chinese community within several hours. On the night of July 7, we called an ad-hoc meeting of all the community groups, and decided to form the General Relief Committee. [18]

Leftist groups—including representatives of the Anti-Imperialist Alliance, the Unemployed Council, and the Chinese Workers' Center—visited the Nationalist government consulate in New York to exchange ideas about the common tasks ahead, as well as to express their loyalty to the government and their support of the cause of national resistance. In so doing, the Chinese left clearly acknowledged that factional conflicts had to cease in order to concentrate on the struggle for national independence and that, for the same reason, the formal leadership of the Nanking Nationalist government and its ruling party, the KMT, had to be accepted. Chinatown was able to maintain this state of unity and peace for almost six years.

The first task in the general mobilization of the community was to establish a General Relief Committee to oversee and coordinate all patriotic activities, particularly fund-raising and propaganda. The committee was sponsored by all the major groups in Chinatown, and its nineteen-member executive council was broadly representative of the community. The community in turn viewed the committee as the pre-eminent relief organization, and as such endowed it with extensive powers. In the area of fund-raising, for example, it was authorized to impose a compulsory monthly contribution on every Chinese person and business in the metropolitan New York area. Although amounts varied according to ability to pay, the minimum was $5, and those who failed to make their scheduled contributions were fined. In serious cases of nonpayment, names might be published in local papers, or the storefront windows of delinquent businesses smeared with eggs. A total of thirty thousand Chinese, according to the official count, contributed every month in the metropolitan New York area. Within six months, the committee announced that it had collected $1 million. In addition, individuals were requested to contribute funds for buying drugs, winter clothing, and other supplies needed by the troops.

Although the committee was the official fund-raising organization, other groups were encouraged to extend the scope of the drive. The Women's Patriotic Association, for instance, sold "patriotic bonds" on the streets of Chinatown, reportedly with great success. The Chinese Hand Laundry Alliance was an especially active participant in the war effort. Some of its young members even set up a flying school and hired a U.S. Army air force major to coach them at a Brooklyn airfield, in the hope of going to China as volunteers. As for fund-raising, the CHLA pioneered the monthly contribution system, trying it out among its own members before it was adopted by the whole community. The CHLA also conceived of the idea of soliciting funds through "donation boxes," which were to be passed around from store to store. It was from such donations that the CHLA was able to purchase three ambulances to send back to China; each vehicle had the alliance's name printed on the sides to boost the troops' morale. During a parade in honor of the Chinese resistance, the CHLA put one of the newly acquired ambulances at the head of the march, thus reminding onlookers of the harsh reality of the war and encouraging further contributions.

NEW YORK'S CHINESE AND "PEOPLE'S DIPLOMACY"

In addition to making financial contributions to the anti-Japanese struggle, Chinese-Americans instituted what they called "people's diplomacy," reaching out to the U.S. people for their support. Until the United States declared war on Japan in 1941, it remained officially "neutral," although relations between the two countries had been tense ever since World War I. Japan's expanding influence in the Far East threatened U.S. interests in the area, and the government gave repeated indications of its displeasure at Japanese aggression in China. In some quarters, too, there was considerable alarm over Japan's close association with the German and Italian fascist governments, and the U.S. leftists were particularly concerned over Japan's use of anti-Communist ideology to justify its attacks on the Soviet Union and China. Thus there was already some recognition that U.S. support for China was needed in order to check the expansion of Japan and, by extension, to combat the worldwide menace of fascism.

It cannot be said, however, that these sentiments were shared by the general public. On the one hand, there was still a strong isolationist tendency in the United States; on the other, many U.S. businesses had commercial and financial interests in Japan and Manchuria, with such giant corporations as Ford, General Motors, Kodak, and Singer engaged in joint operations with Japanese firms.[19]

On the most general level, then, the task of "people's diplomacy" was simply to tell the public what was going on in China and to explain the reasons for the war against Japan. The hope was that once people were informed, they would get involved in concrete actions to aid China, not only by raising funds, but by pressuring U.S. policymakers to move away from their "neutral" stance. Since the U.S. public was far from homogeneous, a whole range of "diplomats" was needed to address the various sectors. Fortunately, there was already a natural division of labor in the Chinese community, for groups representing different political persuasions had also had different sorts of contacts with U.S. society. Leftist and working people's organizations, such as the Anti-Imperialist Alliance and the CHLA, sought support among U.S. left and labor groups, while the CCBA and the KMT appealed to the elites— politicians, businessmen, and church leaders.

One of the first activities calling for public support was a boycott of Japanese goods. The Chinese left approached its U.S. contacts with the idea, and on October 7, 1937, some 15,000 people, including 2,000 Chinese, attended an "Aid China" rally sponsored by the U.S. Congress Against War and Fascism and the Friends of China Committee. The boycott was endorsed by the rally participants; other groups then joined, including the CIO, whose secretary-general called the boycott "a manifestation of the American people's anger toward Japanese aggression in China."[20]

Two months later, the New York Friends of China Committee organized a demonstration to ask women not to buy Japanese silk stockings. Two thousand women, including 450 Chinese, marched down Fifth Avenue carrying banners reading "We'd Rather Wear Cotton Stockings than Silk Ones." Many movie stars, including Loretta Young, Sylvia Sidney, and Frances Farmer, actively participated in promoting the boycott, and many women began to wear cotton stockings, or none at all.

But the Chinese in the United States devoted their greatest energy to stopping U.S. companies from selling scrap iron—which could be converted into military hardware—to Japan. With support from friends in the labor movement, the Chinese set up pickets at piers from which cargo ships were known to take scrap iron. The National Maritime Union supported the boycott, and even its president, Joseph Curran, picketed at Brooklyn's Bush Terminal. Similar demonstrations were organized in San Francisco, and in one instance the longshoremen refused to load the scrap iron onto a departing ship.[21]

In 1938, many Chinese came out in support of the Republican faction in the Spanish Civil War in order to express solidarity with antifascist forces throughout the world. The CHLA was particularly active, sending delegates to a meeting of the U.S. National Democratic and Peace Congress, a progressive antifascist organization. Indeed, the CHLA official representative stated his case so eloquently that the congress elected him to its executive committee.[22]

With the rise of a national consciousness among Chinese in the United States, a new image began to be projected to the general public. For the first time, instead of "tong wars" and internal divisions, unity had been achieved in the community; for the first time, the supposedly "docile" Chinese were reaching out aggressively for support from U.S. society.

WORLD WAR II AND THE CHINESE
IN THE UNITED STATES

In 1941, the United States joined the war on the same side as China, fighting the Axis powers. Backward and semicolonial China suddenly became an ally; the Chinese people suddenly became heroic fighters against fascism. Chiang Kai-shek made the front cover of *Time* as "Man of the Year." As historian Harold Isaacs pointed out in his book *Scratches on Our Minds*, because China's antifascist policy coincided with U.S. objectives at the time, the attitude toward China underwent a dramatic change, from "contempt" to "admiration."[23]

The new image of China affected the status of Chinese in the United States. Before the war, they had complained repeatedly about the preferential treatment accorded Japanese nationals in this country. The magazine *Chinese Student Monthly*, published in the United States, gave one example of this disparity:

> Immigration officials purposely insult the Chinese by treating them unequally . . . when passenger ships disembark, the officials process first class passengers, then second class, then third class, but among the third class the officials invariably process the Japanese before the Chinese. . . . This is clearly because of China's weak international standing as a virtual colony of great powers.

Another article in the same magazine claimed that at the New York Immigration Office, "The average number of Japanese held for investigation in any one week is about three, while an average of twenty Chinese are held, yet the number of incoming Chinese in each week is not much higher than the number of Japanese."[24]

In the early 1940s, the Chinese and Japanese positions were suddenly reversed. The loyalty of Japanese-Americans became suspect, and they were placed in concentration camps for the duration of the war. At the same time, there was active lobbying to improve conditions for the Chinese, and pressure was put on Congress to revoke the Chinese Exclusion Act. When the act was finally repealed in 1943, the Chinese could legally immigrate to the United States for the first time since 1882, even though the quota was a mere 105 people a year.

As important as this higher social status was the improvement in job opportunities. The war demanded a massive mobilization in all industries related to national defense, and minority group workers, including the Chinese, began to enter new fields of employment. President Roosevelt issued an executive order calling for an end to racial discrimination, declaring that it is "only through the unity of all people that we can successfully win the war, regardless of race, color, and creed."[25] The Chinese, formerly denied access to the industrial labor force as well as to most white-collar jobs, were suddenly released from the low-paying service "ghetto" to which they had been restricted. Jobs in factories, shipyards, offices, and laboratories gave them the opportunity to learn new skills, and enabled employers to learn how capable Chinese workers could be. In the long run, this experience helped dispel prejudice among some employers, who continued to hire Chinese after the war.

During the war itself, most Chinese were in the army. One New York City survey showed that approximately 40 percent (13,000) of the Chinese population was drafted, the highest of all national groupings.[26] The reason was an ironic one: because of the Exclusion Act, most Chinese had no dependents and according to the law were the first called. Yet many Chinese actually welcomed military service, anticipating that the special skills they would learn in the army would be useful in civilian life and that, as veterans, they would enjoy many benefits denied them in the past.

The process of integration into the U.S. labor market, which began at this time and which was immeasurably helped by the changed U.S.-China relationship, is a development that is particularly well illustrated by the experience of the Chinese seamen, to which I now turn.

5
PIONEERS IN INTEGRATION: THE CHINESE SEAMEN, 1911-1946

There is very little about the seamen in the literature of the Chinese in the United States, partly because seamen comprise such a mobile group that they are not usually seen as community members. China had no merchant marine of its own, so Chinese seamen had always sought employment on foreign vessels. Those who worked on U.S. ships frequently visited New York on shore leave, or stayed over between tours of duty. Many came to consider New York their home, even though they came from China, and when they were between jobs or unemployed they often sought work in Chinatown, sometimes as waiters; there was then a constant flow of seamen in and out of the area. But although the seamen were mobile, they nevertheless constituted a significant part of the community. Several district associations were composed mainly of seamen, and a number of clubhouses were used as dormitories for those in transit.

Another reason for the scarcity of written material on Chinese seamen is that many of them stayed in the United States as "jumped-ship" aliens, hiding their identity and relying on protection from the community. There are no reliable data as to their numbers; most of the Chinese community, anxious to avoid exposing them, have been reluctant to yield much information. Nevertheless, there are indications that these illegal seamen constituted a significant portion of Chinatown's population. For one thing, the community showed marked uneasiness whenever there was a call for alien registration or an immigration inspection; for another, the tongs were very powerful in Chinatown, and their strength was usually a direct result of the size of the alien "underground."

The seamen, then, were a major part of the working population in New York's Chinatown, and were also the workers most significantly affected by the U.S. labor movement. In the 1930s, the active participation of many Chinese seamen in the National Maritime Union was a breakthrough for Chinese integration into the U.S. working class. Even before that, though, Chinese seamen had a long history of militancy and a high level of class consciousness.

CHINESE SEAMEN AND THE EARLY YEARS OF LABOR ACTIVISM

Since the seamen had traveled to foreign countries and been exposed to advanced or radical ideas, they tended to be more politically aware than other workers, and they played a leading role in the emergence of the labor movement in China in the 1920s. Moreover, because they were from a weak nation, they were constantly exposed to the humiliation of discrimination and tended to be patriotic. As early as 1911, Chinese seamen in Liverpool organized a collective to fight against racial discrimination by British sailors.[1] And even earlier, seamen who worked on foreign vessels had joined the Tung-meng Hui, the revolutionary party formed by Sun Yat-sen to overthrow the Ch'ing Dynasty. The seamen, because of their mobility, were exceedingly useful as agitators and fund-raisers in the overseas Chinese communities. In 1913, in recognition of their high political potential, Dr. Sun created a special organization for them. This group, known as the Overseas Communication Department of the Lien Yi Society, was to be integrated into the revolutionary party, the forerunner of the KMT.

Lien Yi, as a political arm of the KMT, set up party cells on ships that carried large Chinese crews. These cells not only performed trade-union functions, fighting for higher wages and better working conditions, but took up the issue of the seamen's exploitation by the Chinese labor contractors who worked for the shipping companies. Moreover, their members were political educators and agitators, recruiting for the KMT and urging Chinese seamen to support progressive "national" movements.

In 1922, when 50,000 Chinese seamen in Hong Kong demanded higher wages from the British shipping companies, the strike sparked off the nationwide anti-imperialist movement in China. For two months the strike tied up 166 ships, representing 16 steamship companies, and its successful outcome inspired similar actions against other foreign-owned companies. In the celebrated Canton–Hong Kong general strike of 1925–1926, called to protest Britain's senseless slaughter of demonstrating Chinese workers in Shanghai, the seamen were the first to walk off the job. Others followed, and eventually some 200,000 workers went out; Hong Kong harbor was completely paralyzed for nearly a year. Furthermore, the seamen were clearly the most resolute of the strikers. Their action lasted longest and spread farthest, from Canton to Chinese coastal seaports as far north as Tientsin.[2] The head of the General Strike Committee, which coordinated the different labor groups, was Ssu Chao-jen, the seaman who had led the 1922 strike.

With the open split between Communists and Nationalists in 1927, there was no longer any active labor organizing on the part of the KMT, while the CCP was driven into the rural underground. Without the organized leadership of a political party, the seamen lost their direction and reverted to their traditional loyalties. Lien Yi collapsed, and with it the seamen's capacity to struggle against poor working conditions and racial discrimination on foreign vessels.

U.S. UNIONS AND CHINESE SEAMEN

During the Great Depression, with thousands of native seamen unemployed, the U.S. shipping companies often preferred to hire foreign crews, including many Chinese. The advantage lay in the conditions imposed on these crewmen. They were forced to sign a contract that allowed the company to withhold 50 percent of their wages until discharge and they had to post a $500 bond to guarantee compliance. In addition, each seaman had to sign a statement:

We the undersigned, —————, the Chinese crew of the S.S. —————, hereby agree with the captain that we will not join any association of any kind, or attempt to form any associations while around the vessel; if any such association should by founded, it is hereby understood that such men will be returned to Hong Kong at their own expense.[3]

Clearly, then, shipping companies that hired Chinese rather than U.S. seamen could pay a lower wage and expect a "trouble-free" crew. In an all-too-familiar pattern, the Seamen's International Union (SIU), an AFL affiliate, chose to direct its anger at the Chinese seamen instead of the companies. In January 1933, when the "S.S. Lincoln," a Dollar Shipping Company vessel, reached New York harbor, the SIU protested the use of Chinese seamen and demanded their immediate discharge. The union also arranged for the Immigration Office to arrest the Chinese for illegal entry and confine them to Ellis Island; two or three hundred were ultimately deported. The SIU then pressed Congress to pass a bill barring all foreign seamen from working on U.S. ships, claiming that "Chinese seamen charge low wages, thus taking away jobs from Americans."[4]

While this racist attitude toward the Chinese (which extended also to blacks and to other foreigners) was perhaps its worst aspect, the SIU was generally a corrupt and ineffective "company" union. Many of its officials may actually have been paid by the owners *not* to organize. The seamen's wages were low, and there was no limit on working hours, yet the SIU made no effort to win better conditions for its membership. Union officials were unwilling to use the strike as a weapon; they were content simply to collect dues and other "fringe benefits" (in order to get ship assignments, seamen had to pay union officials on the side). And if there were any complaints from members, the union kept them in line through gang violence.[5]

Gradually, some SIU members realized that they could not change the union from within. As they gained support, they resolved to form a new labor organization, the National Maritime Union (NMU), which within a few years became the largest maritime union in the United States.

The new union, in contrast to the SIU, was to be run along scrupulously democratic lines, with national conventions held every other year and officials elected in alternate years. Members were required to vote, and elections were supervised by the Honest Ballot Association. Attendance at union meetings was made compulsory to assure continued rank-and-file control. The most unusual feature in the constitution was a clause providing that there be "no discrimination against any union member because of his race, color, political affiliation, creed, religion, or national origin."[6] The NMU's leaders understood that a strike could be successful only if shipowners were unable to recruit strikebreakers, usually minority-group workers, from elsewhere. By promising racial equality and equal participation, they hoped to encourage potential scabs to join the union rather than work for the companies against their own long-term interests. With this understanding, Ferdinand Smith, a black union leader and later vice-president, was able to convince some 20,000 black seamen, primarily stationed in southern and Gulf ports, to join the 1936–1937 seamen's strike.[7] Without their cooperation, the nationwide strike would surely have failed.

THE 1936–1937 SEAMEN'S STRIKE
AND ITS AFTERMATH

At the time of the 1936–1937 strike, many Chinese were employed on U.S. vessels, but they occupied the most menial positions—usually as cooks or stewards—and were paid an average of $45 per month, as compared to $60 for U.S. seamen. When the NMU called the strike, thousands of Chinese seamen were stranded in New York; without an organization of their own, they had no idea how to deal with the situation. Some of them, resentful about their wretched working conditions, were vaguely sympathetic to the strike; others, however, for a variety of reasons—memories of past racial discrimination, fear of retaliation from the shipping companies, suspicions that the striking seamen were Communists—were reluctant to walk out.

It was at this time that a group of politically active Chinese seamen, disheartened by the lack of leadership, decided to revive the New York Lien Yi Society. This provided an opening for the NMU's New York strike committee, whose representatives promptly approached Lien Yi, urging its members to join the strike. Lien Yi officials were cautious at first, pointing out that the Chinese had special problems. The shipping companies still held the $500 bonds of a number of seamen; moreover, as "aliens," many of them did not even have the right to land in U.S. ports. If they joined the strike, the companies could retaliate by confiscating the bonds and instituting deportation proceedings. After some discussion, Lien Yi made an offer: the Chinese would join the strike in return for NMU support in presenting the companies with three demands: (1) equal treatment of the Chinese; (2) their right to shore leave; and (3) an equal wage scale.[8] The NMU readily agreed.

The two organizations were of one mind; now the seamen themselves had to be convinced. Lien Yi held mass meetings to explain the importance of the strike and how its success would benefit the Chinese. The NMU, in turn, asked all Chinese seamen with U.S. citizenship to get off the ships and join the picket lines; it tried to get permission for noncitizens to come ashore as well, asking the Chinese consulate to negotiate with the Immigration Office over the matter. It promised that if any Chinese lost their jobs because of participation in the strike, all of them—citizens or not—would have an equal opportunity of employment after the strike was over. During its negotiations with management, the NMU also demanded equal pay for Chinese seamen.

Reassured by all these guarantees, about three thousand Chinese seamen joined Lien Yi and participated in the strike; for the first time, Chinese workers became a part of the U.S. labor movement. The strike was certainly a success from the NMU's point of view; as for the Chinese seamen, while the experience gave them a new sense of militancy, they still had their own specific problems to solve.

The matter of shore leave continued to be one of their most urgent concerns. According to U.S. immigration rules, all foreign sailors except the Chinese had this right, as long as they could produce proof of their status as seamen; fines were imposed on any shipping company that violated the regulation.[9] The rationale was that the Chinese seamen couldn't be trusted not to jump ship and remain in this country, and while it is true that some of them did just that, the majority were career sailors who bitterly resented the racist implications and injustice of the immigration ruling.

A new problem arose in 1936, when Congress authorized federal subsidies to shipping companies carrying the U.S. mail—on the condition that these ships hired no foreign seamen. Since the Chinese were practically the only foreigners working on U.S. ships at the time, it would not be an exaggeration to call the act an attack on them. And it was effective: Chinese workers were systematically laid off by the shipping companies—fired with no warning, dropped off at any convenient port, and left to make their own way home.

The Chinese seamen, better organized and more militant than ever before, moved to confront these issues. Seamen on the "S.S. President Taft," owned by the Dollar Shipping Company, sounded the first protest. When the ship arrived in New York harbor on

June 16, 1937, they went on a sit-down strike to protest the shipping company's discriminatory treatment of Chinese, the layoffs in particular. This act of defiance immediately won the backing of the Chinese community, and enthusiastic reports were published in the local papers. Chinese seamen on the "S.S. Polk," also in the harbor, went on a sympathy strike. Most significant of all, the NMU declared full support for the Chinese seamen's three demands: (1) that all Chinese seamen be allowed shore leave; (2) that the shipping companies offer six months' compensatory pay; and (3) that all seamen who had been laid off be guaranteed return passage. After two days, the Dollar Shipping Company agreed to negotiate. With the NMU giving tactical advice to the Chinese, the company agreed to pay a six-month compensatory salary to those who were laid off, and to rehire all those who had participated in the sit-down strike.[10]

Even though the company did not give in to all the demands, the agreement represented a tremendous advance, as did the strike itself. Undertaken on the workers' own initiative and backed by the sympathy strike, the action revealed a growing sense of solidarity and political consciousness among Chinese seamen. Yet the seamen's organization remained under the control of the KMT, and local party leaders were disquieted by the radicalization of Chinese seamen in New York. The KMT was suspicious of any Chinese involvement in labor struggles, and was particularly distrustful of the NMU. Lien Yi, as a political arm of the party, concentrated on gaining the seamen's support for the KMT against its internal opposition in China. Since it was interested in controlling the members, not in dealing with their on-the-job problems, it decided to purge all radical elements from the organization. Even this, however, could not stop the militants: they promptly formed a new group, the Chinese Seamen's Patriotic Association, which continued to work closely with the NMU; Lien Yi sunk once again into decline.

The Chinese seamen found the NMU a worthy ally, not only in its labor struggles but in the political arena as well. Its leaders were men who had always been strong opponents of fascist dictatorship; in 1934, even before the union was founded, they had refused to sail on ships bound for Italy because of that country's aggression against Ethiopia. Then, in 1936, some NMU members joined the Republican side in the Spanish Civil War; 221 U.S. seamen—a large number from the NMU—were eventually killed in the struggle. The official NMU journal, *Pilot*, repeatedly warned that a fascist victory in Spain would lead to a new world war, instigated by the Nazis.[11] It is not surprising, then, that in 1937 the NMU also came out in support of China's war of resistance, joining Chinese seamen in refusing to ship scrap iron to Japan. The union's identification with China's cause was particularly significant, for the majority of people in the United States were not yet alert to the menace of worldwide fascism. As late as 1940, many major newspapers—unlike the NMU's *Pilot*—continued to advocate U.S. neutrality.

WORLD WAR II AND THE CHINESE SEAMEN

In 1939, within a few months of the start of World War II, Hitler's forces overran most of the western part of Europe, isolating England. Although the United States had not formally taken sides, it was providing supplies to the beseiged nation, principally on U.S. and British cargo vessels. Many ships were sunk by German U-boats patrolling the North Atlantic, and seamen suffered extremely high casualties.

In December 1941, the United States formally entered the war. Two of its allies, England and the Soviet Union, were under attack by Germany, and President Roosevelt initiated a Lend-Lease program to ship them weapons and supplies. As convoys of these "Liberty" ships crossed the Atlantic, German U-boats intensified their attacks, and large numbers of men and vessels were lost. By the end of 1942, the first year of U.S. participation in the war, almost 4 percent of all U.S. merchant seamen were dead or missing—four times the combined losses of the army, navy, marine corps, and coast guard during the same period.[12]

These high casualties and the growth of war-associated shipping activity created a sudden need for sailors. Previous restrictions against the use of foreigners had to be relaxed, and Chinese seamen were rehired. By the early 1940s, 15,000 were serving in the U.S. merchant marine, and many on British ships as well. As a result, the treatment of Chinese seamen became an increasingly important issue.

The major problem was an old one that had never been resolved: the question of shore leave for non-U.S. citizens. U.S. authorities still refused to grant shore leave to noncitizen Chinese, and some sailors remained on the Atlantic Ocean for months without setting foot on land. The war, however, gave the Chinese some leverage: here were thousands of seamen who were taking the same risks for the Allied cause, yet were denied equal treatment. Chinese seamen appealed to various authorities, while the NMU helped out with a public statement in support of their right to shore leave and ran an article in the *Pilot* urging equal treatment for all seamen.[13] In 1942, six Chinatown community groups held a public forum urging U.S. authorities to change the ruling. The U.S. Justice Department finally gave all seamen working on Allied ships the right to shore leave, a significant advance in the Chinese battle against racial discrimination.

The Chinese government made no effort to help the seamen in their struggle, and when they finally triumphed, their own consulate insultingly warned them not to use their newly gained right to "jump ship."[14] As we shall see, the home government was equally unsupportive of the still more difficult struggle of Chinese seamen on British ships.

Because there were many Chinese seamen working on the British ships that docked at New York during the war, their situation was also a matter of concern to the Chinatown community. These sailors, often hired in Hong Kong, were sometimes recruited by deceitful means, with British shipping companies telling them they would be serving along the China coast, then sending them to the Atlantic instead.[15] They were also paid much lower salaries than their British counterparts (a weekly average of £4–10, as compared to £15–20), and there were numerous reports of harsh treatment—for instance, officers beating and jailing the Chinese and then docking their pay.

When the Chinese seamen demanded equal treatment, they were met with refusals and violence. One Chinese seaman who had been so abused that he requested to be relieved of duty and put ashore was shot and killed by a British captain for "insubordination."[16] New York's Chinese community learned of the incident and several groups protested to the British government; the response was that officers had the right to "discipline" seamen under war conditions. This left no recourse but desertion, and when many Chinese left their ships in New York City, the British companies demanded that the U.S. Immigration Office find and arrest them. The immigration authorities started a door-to-door search, and for weeks on end there were middle-of-the-night raids.[17] The community was shaken and outraged at this violation of their rights, regarding it as an insult to all Chinese. The Committee for the Protection of the Foreign Born, a U.S. civil liberties group, lodged a protest with the immigration authorities, accusing them of harassing Chinese residents and abusing their rights. Typically, the Chinese government made no move to help.

The raids netted some four hundred seamen, many of whom refused to go back to work on British vessels unless conditions improved. The British attitude toward this may be gauged by one spokesman's comment that "the only way to get the Chinese to work and to leave the U.S.A. is to get tough. . . . Most of the deserters don't want to work. . . . The seamen were coolies before they became seamen and they are still coolies."[18] On the other hand, there were many who felt the Chinese deserters were justified. The *Shanghai Evening Post & Mercury,* a U.S.-owned English-language paper that had moved to the United States at the outbreak of the war, printed several articles urging public support for the seamen's cause, and most of the local Chinese papers also gave them extensive coverage. On the labor front, the NMU defended them, as did the International Seamen's Alliance in London.

The situation, however, was complicated by a number of jurisdictional problems. The Chinese seamen were neither British nor U.S. citizens. When they deserted in New York, they were not even employees of U.S. companies. The U.S. government could arrest them as illegal aliens, but it could not deal with their original complaints. As Chinese nationals, the seamen should have been represented by the Chinese government, which could have settled the dispute through diplomatic channels, but even after repeated urging it refused to become involved.

As for the Chinese seamen who continued to work on British vessels, they had no organized representation. Those who had not already been arrested could not organize for fear that they would be. Without an official representative, they had no one to help them. U.S. labor organizations could exert moral pressure on the British, but they could not negotiate directly with management. As the president of the NMU commented,

> The American seamen's union tried to help the Chinese many times. The union had supported the principle of equality of all seamen, but on the Chinese side there is no seamen's organization, and there is no true spokesman for them. . . . The union could not give too much help under these circumstances.[19]

In 1943, a group of concerned Chinese seamen got together and formed the Chinese Seamen's Union to represent those who worked for the British. Before the union could even begin to function, however, Lien Yi was claiming that it was Communist-controlled and not a true representative of the Chinese seamen, while the local KMT papers insisted the use of the word "Chinese" in its name was "illegitimate" because the union could not claim to represent all Chinese.[20] Under these circumstances, the Chinese Seamen's Union was unable to negotiate effectively with the British.

As it turned out, however, its efforts had already been circumvented by a secret deal between the Chinese government and the British companies. In this, the government was motivated not by any great concern for the seamen's plight, but by pressure from the British, who were impatient with the shipping delays caused by desertions. It was agreed that all Chinese who deserted and were caught would be deported from the United States and sent to serve in India—scarcely a humane decision but one which stood, despite protests from Chinese community groups and U.S. sympathizers.

The attitude of the Chinese government was revealed in a conversation between the Chinese consul-general and a group of seamen threatened with deportation to India:

> Our government did a great many things for you people, but you seamen, by demanding equal treatment, caused many ship delays. Venerable Chiang [Chiang Kai-shek] was very angry with all of you. National interests should be primary. We will not allow a small group of seamen to destroy our friendship with Britain. We want you people to go back and serve on the ship. If you refuse, you will be sent to India for service. I hope you will cooperate with us and all of us will be happy.[21]

There was a clear lesson in this for other Chinese seamen in New York: they could not expect any support from China. If they wanted equality, they could get it only by fighting on the same side as U.S. workers.

THE CHINESE SEAMEN AND THE NMU

The incidents involving Chinese seamen on British ships led more of their counterparts on U.S. vessels to join the NMU. Chinese membership increased from 1,000 in 1942 to 3,000 in 1946; a Chinese section was set up, and it played an active role in the union.

The NMU spoke out constantly on issues concerning its Chinese members. In 1943, it officially supported the repeal of the Chinese Exclusion Act. In 1944, it asked Congress to pass legislation giving the right of naturalization to all foreign seamen who had worked on U.S. vessels for more than three years during the war. Although this proposal was never approved, in August 1945 the Department of Transportation did allow noncitizen Chinese seamen to continue to work on U.S. ships if they had been hired before July 30, 1945.[22] Thousands benefited from this ruling, and the union's tireless efforts generally resulted in increased hiring of Chinese seamen, citizen and noncitizen, on U.S. vessels in the postwar period.

The NMU also called repeatedly for the cessation of the civil war in China and urged the establishment of a coalition government; later, it condemned the continued presence of U.S. troops in China and their interference in the internal conflicts of that country. It was obvious that these positions closely reflected the sentiments of the union's Chinese members. The Chinese section, in turn, supported the union in its activities on behalf of all seamen. In 1946, the NMU called a strike for higher wages. To ensure that as many of their countrymen as possible would join the walkout, the Chinese immediately formed a strike committee, whose executive council included representatives from the seven districts in China that most of the seamen came from. Since the end of the war, the committee reminded the seamen, the wages of all seamen had generally declined drastically, and those who did menial work below deck—and that applied to the majority of Chinese—were the worst off. Further, although nearly six thousand foreign seamen, including many Chinese, had lost their lives in the war, once it was over the Immigration Office began to harass them. The strike committee sent a representative to meet with Chinatown leaders and explain the importance of the strike. It also requested all striking seamen not to seek interim employment in Chinese restaurants, so that the Immigration Office would have no excuse for arresting them; at the same time, it urged the other Chinese in the community not to undermine the seamen's interests by working as scabs for the shipping companies.

Such active participation in the NMU was a step forward not only for the seamen but for all Chinese workers in the United States, laying the foundation for their integration in other areas of the U.S. labor movement. The patriotic movement against Japan brought unity to the community for the first time; it also stimulated contact with the world beyond Chinatown, as the wider society responded to Chinese appeals for support. At the end of World War II, the Chinese in New York seemed on the verge of breaking out of their isolation and exclusion. Yet by the early 1950s, all these gains had been erased—a development that has less to do with the Chinese in the United States than with events in their homeland, specifically the socialist revolution.

6
NEW YORK'S CHINATOWN
AND THE CHINESE REVOLUTION,
1941-1954

THE BREAKDOWN OF THE UNITED FRONT

With the establishment of the united front in China in 1936, the country appeared to be in a favorable position to defeat Japan. It soon became clear, however, that the KMT had no intention of relinquishing its supreme authority. When the Japanese attacked and occupied coastal and other populated areas, the Nationalist government retreated to the hinterlands, beyond the range of enemy troops, and rarely engaged in anti-Japanese activities. At the same time, it cast a suspicious eye on the Communist-led resistance in Japanese-occupied areas, fearing an expansion of CCP territorial control beyond its guerrilla bases in the Yenan region. Military clashes between the CCP and the KMT began in 1938; then, in 1941, some nine thousand Communist troops were surrounded and attacked by Nationalist forces, with thousands of casualties on both sides. This battle marked the end of the second united front.

The CCP and the KMT pursued different strategies throughout the war. The CCP policy, known as "fighting strengthens the resistance," called for constant small-scale guerrilla warfare against the Japanese. Instead of depending on aid and supplies from the Allies, the Communists built up a network of popular support and extended their political influence throughout large areas that were under Japanese control. The KMT, in contrast, called its policy "waiting in preparation" for the ultimate confrontation with the Japanese—which meant, in practice, relying on the Great Powers, especially the United States and the Soviet Union, to prosecute the war. Between 1941 and 1944, Chiang Kai-shek let the Allies hold back the Japanese while he concentrated on his internal enemies. Already looking toward the future, he hoped to establish himself as the dominant force in the postwar China.

Yet the Nationalist government in Chungking, the wartime capital, was corrupt, and its conservative leadership had no desire to democratize the political system. As for the army, its command structure was archaic, its rank-and-file mistreated, ill fed, and undisciplined. Throughout these years of "resistance," the whole thrust of Chiang's policy was to consolidate his own political and military power, and the United States was not pleased by his refusal to make basic reforms and create an effective fighting force. In 1942, in an attempt to encourage Chiang to take a more active role in fighting the Japanese, the Allies made him commander-in-chief of the China theater. Unwittingly, however, they only added another title to a long list that already included generalissimo, president of the Military Commission, chairman of the Executive Yuan and Central Executive Committee of the KMT, and president of the Supreme Committee of the National Government. He even became director-general of the KMT, a "sacred" post left vacant since the death of Sun Yat-sen.

This conflict between Chiang's ambitions and the prosecution of the war created tensions in U.S.-China relations, the effects of which were soon being felt in New York's Chinatown. While the united front lasted longer there than it did in China, by 1943 there were open splits over the proper attitude the Chinese should take toward the U.S. government.

According to the U.S. view, Europe and the South Pacific should be the primary battle fronts; the China theater was secondary, requiring just enough resistance to spread Japanese defenses as thinly as possible. Yet Chiang Kai-shek, though himself unwilling to engage in active combat with the Japanese, nevertheless expected the Allies to make China the focus of their activities. When his constant demands for manpower and supplies were not met, he threatened imminent "collapse" unless additional aid was forthcoming. This was a kind of blackmail, for if China did in fact collapse, it might negotiate a separate settlement with Japan—a disaster for which the Allies, and particularly the United States, would then be held responsible.

In New York's Chinatown, Chiang's "collapse" threat was parroted by the *Chinese Journal*, which had lost its liberal orientation after being bought by the KMT in 1940. Ironically, it was the left wing and progressive elements in the community that defended the U.S. government's stance, which the KMT called a "policy of selling out China." A series of articles in the *China Daily News*, a newly established paper backed by the Chinese Hand Laundry Alliance, accused the KMT of falling into the "enemy's plot of dividing the anti-Japanese allies" and pointed out that the primary responsiblity for resisting Japanese aggression should be borne by the Chinese people themselves.[1]

Then, in late 1943, a serious famine in Kwangtung province was reported in the *New York Times*. Most Chinese in the United States had come originally from Kwangtung, and this came as quite a shock to the community, especially since Nationalist news sources had not discussed the famine at all. After the *Times* report, the local KMT tried to pacify Chinese residents by assuring them that the problem was not serious, and that the government had it under control. But letters from relatives in Kwangtung told a different story. They blamed the famine on corrupt government officials who had joined hands with the merchants and aggravated the scarcity by hoarding food and supplies. The price of rice rose precipitiously, and when Chinese in New York tried to cable funds to relatives, they found the Bank of China slow and inefficient. Moreover, while money cabled home had to be converted at the official rate of $1 to 20 yuan, the much more realistic blackmarket rate was $1 to 100 yuan; thus overseas Chinese had to spend five times the official rate if they were to do their relatives any good.

In a cable to the Nationalist government, the CHLA urged an investigation of official wrongdoing in relation to the Kwangtung famine and recommended severe punishment for the guilty parties. The district associations lent their support to this protest, and a community meeting was called to discuss how to help famine victims. The meeting was well attended, and bitter accusations were voiced against the inaction of government officials.[2] Instead of responding to these charges, the local KMT retaliated with "redbaiting," stigmatizing the CHLA as the agitator and as a Communist organization that was simply using the famine as a weapon against the Nationalist government.

Before the issue of the famine was resolved, there was more bad news from China. In the summer of 1944, while Allied forces were piling up victories in Europe and the South Pacific, the Nationalist army was being handed an equally impressive series of miserable defeats. The Japanese drove KMT troops out of one base after another, and millions of dollars worth of U.S.-supplied weapons and airfield facilities were lost. Yet even such clear evidence of its incompetence turned the Nationalist government not to reform but to a renewed attack on dissenters—a campaign that extended to New York.

One of the targets was Liu Leung-mo, a well-known figure in the community and conductor of Chinatown's Anti-Japanese Patriotic Chorus, who had told a *New York Times* reporter that the Nationalist defeats were largely a result of the government's internal problems. If the government were more democratic and thus had greater popular support, he stated, it could have resolved any problems within the military establishment. Local KMT officials immediately attacked Liu as a Communist and a traitor, and the chorus he had organized was branded a Communist front.

The Nationalist government also sent overseas agents into New York's Chinatown to spy on political dissidents and, if necessary, silence them. After the *China Daily News* published several articles critical of the government, KMT agents told newsvendors not to carry the paper and beat up those who did not comply. Such incidents led a moderate local paper, *Hsin Pao*, to comment that the objects of government persecution should be spies, traitors, and corrupt officials, not honest political dissenters or the patriotic masses and students. [*3]

When the Chinese in New York again tried to send financial aid to their relatives in China, they found the "official" value of their dollars even less realistic than before—now *seventy* times as much money had to be sent home to keep up with the real market rate. Many Chinese' savings were wiped out in their efforts to help, and repeated requests for the reform of the official exchange rate were ignored. An editorial in a Chinatown newspaper asked:

> What have the overseas Chinese done to make the government ignore all of their problems? . . . When we needed help from the government, it paid not the slightest attention to us, and yet when the government needed money, we overseas Chinese always donated generously to them. . . . but what do we get in return? [4]

The Nationalist government was quickly antagonizing its strongest supporters, the expatriate Chinese whose contributions had done so much to support the anti-Japanese resistance.

Many in Chinatown felt that KMT officials had no respect for them because they were uneducated workers. In 1945, the United Nations was founded in San Francisco; when the Nationalist representative to the ceremony, T. V. Soong, paid a visit to New York, he stayed at a luxury hotel and refused invitations to speak in Chinatown. In contrast, the CCP representative to the UN conference, Tung Pi-wu, who was in San Francisco, spoke at many community-sponsored meetings. This was not lost on New York's Chinese, and when it came time to consider China's future in the postwar world, few among them saw any merit in a continuation of the KMT's autocratic rule.

---

*According to a *New York Times* report, Chinese students at Harvard University were told by a Nationalist agent that their course selections and majors had to be approved by local party representatives. The *Times* called this an outrageous attempt at "thought control."

As the end of the war drew closer, tensions between the KMT and the CCP increased. The KMT had no intention of relinquishing its dominant position, while the CCP, with the popular support it had cultivated during the war, was not about to be left out of any future government. Mao Tse-tung, chairman of the Communist Party, called for the formation of a coalition government in which there would be no place for Chiang's personal dictatorship; the generalissimo, in turn, was prepared to fight the Communists to maintain his rule. Most Chinese wanted peace, not civil war, and a compromise on both sides.

Most of New York's Chinese, too, favored a coalition government. The CHLA was the first group to publicly urge its establishment. It sent telegrams to the Nationalist government in Chungking and the Communist Party in Yenan, calling for serious negotiations and the avoidance of a one-party dictatorship. The CHLA was inspired not so much by ideology as by a simple desire for peace, and the performance of the Nationalist government during the war years was certainly no advertisement for the virtues of a single-party regime. A newspaper owned by the conservative Chih-kun tong, which had no love for either the KMT or the CCP, also came out in support of a coalition government and sent cables to Chungking and Yenan:

> We are uniformly and absolutely against the resumption of civil war. Our organization proposed the commencing of a national conference attended by all political parties to jointly discuss the future of China. We urge the formation of a coalition government based on a constitution with democratic principles.[5]

But perhaps the sentiments of the community were best expressed in *Hsin Pao:*

> We the people sincerely hope that the two sides will continue to negotiate until a format for cooperation can be found. . . . It will

be most harmful to the interests of the Chinese people as a whole if these negotiations are not started as soon as possible and a delay will also be detrimental to each of the two parties.[6]

In September 1945 Japan surrendered and New York's Chinatown celebrated with a parade and victory demonstrations. Thousands made plans to return to China to visit relatives, to retire, to start business ventures, or to seek wives to bring back to the United States. In China, the KMT and CCP armies began a mad rush to reconquer the Japanese-occupied areas. The clash was sharpest in Manchuria, the industrial center of the country. The United States stepped in to mediate, but Chiang felt no need to make serious concessions. Despite his lack of success against the Japanese, he was confident that his army, with U.S.-trained troops, heavy equipment, and an air force, had a clear advantage over the Communists.

Despite Chiang's optimism, the contest in Manchuria, and in North China generally, turned out badly for his army. The Communists had set up strong and sophisticated underground networks that were easily converted into an unexpectedly powerful military machine. Chiang requested additional help and the United States transported between 400,000 and 500,000 Nationalist troops to combat locations by air. In addition, 53,000 marines landed in North China to occupy Peking, Tientsin, the Kailan coal mines, and, more crucial, the railway lines in order to "hold political authority in trust for the Chungking Government."[7] By 1946, U.S. military assistance to the Nationalists exceeded $1 billion, and over 120,000 U.S. troops were stationed in China.

The U.S. government persisted in calling this policy one of "noninvolvement" in Chinese domestic affairs, yet to many people it looked like something quite different—and disturbing. The CIO sent cables to the president and secretary of state protesting U.S. armed intervention in the internal affairs of an ally. The president of the NMU publicly denounced such continuing interference, and even staged a one-day work stoppage to demand the immediate return of U.S. troops from China. In fact, acccording to a *New*

York Post reader's survey published on August 27, 1946, withdrawal seemed to be what the majority of people wanted.

THE CIVIL WAR IN CHINA

When civil war resumed in 1946, few in New York's Chinatown welcomed the news, and there were misgivings about the role the United States was playing, even among members of the KMT. A message protesting U.S. intervention in China, signed by the CHLA, the Chinese Youth Club, individual members of New York's KMT and its youth organization, the Three People's Principles Youth Corps, was sent to President Truman.

Chiang Kai-shek's troops were no match for the Red Army, poorly armed as it was. Unable to win either battles or popular support, Chiang was forced to retreat from one area after another. Continued incompetence and corruption brought further economic disintegration, and astronomical inflation. The yen was devalued sixty-seven times between January 1946 and August 1948; it became so unstable that gold and foreign currency were increasingly used instead. A "currency reform" was instituted, replacing the old coinage with the "gold yuan." A price ceiling was set, and private hoarding of foreign currency or gold was strictly forbidden. Two thousand people were "executed" for violating this law. The Chinese people converted their liquid assets into gold yuan; when it too collapsed, in 1948, millions found themselves penniless.[8] After that, few remained loyal to the Nationalist government.

Yet still the regime survived and its agents continued to plague New York's Chinese community. To silence student dissent, KMT spies threatened to revoke passports; they also disrupted peaceful gatherings for political discussion. The local reaction to all this? Quite similar to what A. Doak Barnett, author of *China on the Eve of Communist Takeover*, had observed as the general feeling in

China at the time: "Any change will be for the better: this can't go on."[9] Or, as a *Hsin Pao* editorial described it:

> Most of us overseas Chinese are nonpartisan by nature. Even though some of us joined political parties, we did it largely for patriotic reasons. Our political emotions may be very intense, but they are full of pure intentions. For, after all, none of us expect to become government officials, or expect any special recognition. Whenever China faces problems, we are always able to put aside the differences we have here and unite to help our country; recent community efforts in support of the resistance against Japan are a good example. . . . When the war against the Japanese ended, we overseas Chinese dearly hoped that the domestic affairs of China could finally get on the right track, but to our dismay large-scale civil war broke out. Most of us neutral observers of the partisan conflicts between the KMT and the CCP had to adjust our evaluations according to the present situation. In the past, the Chinese Communist elements in Chinatown often initiated disruptive activities and caused a great deal of misgivings in the community . . . but in recent years their activities in Chinatown have been more constructive. In contrast, it is the KMT's recent activities that show it to be corrupt and destructive. We have never been satisfied with the Communists, but today we have lost our sympathy for the KMT. This is unfortunate for the KMT.
>
> We feel that both sides are wrong in their unwillingness to resolve their disputes peacefully. But if the KMT insists on a one-party dictatorship and does not allow freedom of speech, no one can give them helpful advice. In that respect, the Communists unwillingness to give up their arms can well be appreciated.[10]

In 1948, Chiang's army lost some 500,000 troops and was defeated at the crucial battle of Hwai-hai; it was now only a matter of time before the Nationalist regime collapsed. New York's Chinatown awaited the installation of a new government, curious as to what its policies would be. They were particularly concerned about the new attitude toward overseas Chinese, and some even went so far as to inquire what the new policy on investment in China would be.[11]

A SWING TO THE RIGHT

While the Chinese in New York were adjusting to the possibility of a Communist regime in China, the United States as a whole was moving to the right. As the leading Western power in the postwar years, the United States viewed the growing strength of the Communist block in Eastern Europe, under the leadership of the Soviet Union, as a major threat to the "democratic" world. On March 12, 1947, the United States intervened in the Greek civil war, thus committing itself to what later became known as the Truman Doctrine—a crusade to halt "Soviet expansionism." It was this anti-Soviet strategy that determined that the U.S. government would finance the postwar reconstruction of Japan and Germany, as well as pour nearly $4 billion worth of arms and equipment into Chiang Kai-shek's regime before its collapse in 1949.

On the domestic front, the Truman administration was equally conservative. In 1947 there was a wave of investigations of "Communism" and denunciations of "Reds." The House Un-American Activities Committee, convened as a permanent congressional body, spearheaded a broad offensive against "radical agitators," "Communist sympathizers," and "fellow travelers." More than 2 million public employees were required to submit to the "loyalty oath program" in order to combat the "Communist menace in America."[12]

The U.S. reaction to developments in China must be seen in this context. For diehard anti-Communists, Chiang Kai-shek could do no wrong—scarcely a rational attitude given the billions of dollars required to maintain him—and Communist rule was unthinkable. The general public simply could not comprehend a "leftward" shift in Chinese communities throughout the United States. But, as an editorial in the China Daily News noted, the real change was not the radicalization of the Chinese community, but "the increasing 'right-ward' leaning of the American political scene," which, the paper warned, "will bring to the overseas Chinese some very difficult problems."[13]

There was some hope in New York's Chinatown that with education, the U.S. public would understand what was going on in China. A few groups tried to promote the idea of nonintervention in Chinese domestic affairs. The Chinese section of the NMU, for example, was able to mobilize U.S. seamen to boycott a shipment of supplies to Chiang. The CHLA sent letters and telegrams asking congressional leaders to vote against military aid to the Nationalist regime. A new China Aid Committee was organized to generate public enthusiasm for a democratic China, and a series of forums were held by the Chinese and their U.S. supporters to discuss the government's policy. Thousands of labor, intellectual, and political leaders attended "speak-outs" against Chiang and the U.S. presence in China. One of the main organizers of these events was the once-famous "Christian general," Fung Yu-shan, himself a KMT member. Originally a big-time warlord and never a Communist, Fung had nevertheless recognized the utter corruption of the Chiang regime and had come to the United States to promote the establishment of a democratic government.

In 1948, the presidential election provided the Chinese with another possible platform for their views. Henry Wallace, who ran on the Progressive Party ticket against Thomas Dewey and Harry Truman, was the only candidate to come out against U.S. intervention in China's domestic affairs. A Chinese Committee to Support Wallace was started in San Francisco's Chinatown and many Chinese in New York also backed his campaign. But Wallace lost and, unfortunately for the Chinese, most of their potential allies—leftist and labor leaders, as well as liberal elements who felt that continued support of Chiang was not in the national interest— were by then themselves under fire. Any who dared to voice their honest opinions about China, whether workers in the State Department, academics, or journalists, were singled out and attacked as "Reds." As veteran journalist George Seldes observed:

> There is fear in Washington, not only among government employees but among the few remaining liberals and democrats who hoped to salvage something in the New Deal. There is fear in

> Hollywood . . . there is fear in the book publishing houses . . .
> there is fear among writers, scientists, school teachers, among all
> who are not part of the reactionary movement.[14]

Chiang Kai-shek's forces took full advantage of this repressive
climate to set up a conservative network, known as the "China
Lobby," in the United States. This group, which included con-
gressmen, military officials, scholars, businessmen, and journalists,
did not confine its activities to procuring assistance for Chiang,
but, with the help of the House Un-American Activities Committee, persecuted its critics. Such respected scholars as Owen
Lattimore, John K. Fairbank, and Lawrence Rosinger were accused
of being "pro-Communist," while the Institute of Pacific Relations,
for years one of the most insightful observers of the Chinese
situation, was said to be "Communist-led." Many of this country's
best-known China specialists—Derk Bode, Edgar Snow, Pearl
Buck, Agnes Smedley, Theodore White—were blacklisted for
their failure to support Chiang.

If the Chinese could get little help from the liberal community,
they could expect even less from the U.S. left and labor movements, which were under even more intense pressure. The Labor-
Management Relations Act of 1947 (more familiarly known as
the Taft-Hartley Act, which outlawed the closed shop, industrywide bargaining, jurisdictional strikes, and monetary contributions by unions for political purposes, and withdrew union rights
from any labor union whose officers failed to sign non-Communist
affidavits) was intended to control trade unionism in America, and
progressive labor leaders were systematically purged.

There was not much that New York's Chinese could do or say
to dissipate this atmosphere of fear and suspicion, and it seemed
to make a mockery of their hopes for further integration into
U.S. society.

THE END OF AN ERA

The weakening of U.S. labor, left, and liberal movements in the late 1940s deprived the Chinatown community of important allies in its struggle to combat the domination of the traditional associations and become part of the U.S. labor force. The promising beginning made in the 1930s appeared hopelessly stalled.

One of the biggest stumbling blocks was the postwar depression. For the Chinese, as for other groups, this set back the cause of racial equality. In 1946, the army stopped accepting black enlistees, while unemployment among blacks and minorities increased at a much faster rate than among whites. In 1946, a Fair Employment Practices Committee report observed that "the wartime employment gains of Negro, Mexican-American and Jewish workers are being lost through an unchecked revival of discriminatory practices."[15] This was equally true of the Chinese, who had won access to industrial jobs for the first time in half a century, only to be denied them now. In the spring of 1946, a group of Chinese workers in New York signaled their rising concern over this postwar "backlash" by attending a citywide rally to protest racial discrimination.[16] The economic depression also fostered resentment against "undesirable" aliens. There was a Justice Department drive to deport "radical" foreign-born residents, including such top union leaders as Ferdinand Smith of the NMU, Charles Doyle of the United Chemical Workers, Henry Podosky of the International Worker's Order, and Harry Bridges of the International Longshoremen's Union.

During the late 1940s, the overseas Chinese labored under the additional disadvantage of being a kind of secondary target for the U.S. government's hostility toward the new regime in China. When the Korean War brought Chinese and U.S. troops into direct confrontation, the loyalty of every Chinese in the United States came under suspicion. U.S. policymakers considered the People's Republic of China the most hostile enemy and the Nationalist government, now on Taiwan, the "legitimate" representative of

China. Since the residents of New York's Chinatown showed little support for Chiang, U.S. authorities automatically assumed they were pro-Communist. Some members of the community were even accused of operating as "Communist" agents; subpoenas were issued and investigations conducted by the FBI and the Immigration Office.

An alarming threat to the Chinese in the United States was posed by the 1950 Internal Security Act (McCarran Act), co-sponsored by Senator Pat McCarran and Representative Richard M. Nixon. This law permitted the president to declare an "internal security emergency" during which the attorney general, in a virtual suspension of *habeas corpus* rights, could "apprehend and detain" any suspects. Since virtually all Chinese in the United States were now considered "suspects" because of the direct involvement of the People's Republic in the Korean War, the act could have been used to incarcerate the entire overseas Chinese community. After all, there was a precedent in the mass imprisonment of Japanese-Americans during World War II.

The McCarran Act made it mandatory to exclude aliens who were or had at any time been members of the Communist Party. The Immigration Office used this act extensively against Chinese with "radical" or "progressive" views. One example was the case of Kwong Hai-chew, a Chinese seaman who had been a legal U.S. resident since 1945. On returning to this country following a tour of duty on a U.S. merchant vessel, Kwong was denied re-entry on the grounds of his alleged membership in the Communist Party between 1945 and 1948. Under cross-examination by the defense attorney, prosecution witnesses were unable to substantiate this charge, but because Kwong was indeed an activist—known as a progressive leader in the Chinese section of the NMU and elected chairman (over a conservative pro-KMT candidate) of a Chinese seamen's association—it took seventeen years of litigation to reverse the decision to deport him.[17]

While there was no wholesale detention of the Chinese under the McCarran Act, harassment continued on a number of fronts.

In 1951, for example, nine U.S.-educated Chinese students, specialists in the technical sciences, were on their way home when they were stopped by U.S. authorities and ordered to leave their ship at Honolulu. The students' advanced scientific training, it was explained, would be used by the Communist government against U.S. interests. In the following years, 150 more U.S.-educated students and scholars were subjected to similar treatment, and the detention order was not lifted until the summer of 1955.[18]

Probably the most extreme expression of the anti-Chinese climate of the 1950s was the 1955 Drumright Report. It charged that the falsification of documents by Chinese immigrants from Hong Kong constituted massive fraud, and that Communist agents were using these illegal channels to infiltrate the United States. As a result, the State and Justice departments imposed unusually stringent requirements on all Chinese entering this country—as if they were to be assumed guilty of "fakery" unless they could prove their innocence.

While there was illegal immigration, it was scarcely sufficient to justify either the report or the general feeling of distrust that followed in its wake. "Passports for Sale, an Old Chinese Racket Bothers U.S." screamed the title of a sensationalized article in *U.S. News & World Report*. "Thousands of Chinese in recent years have obtained illegal entry into the U.S. by posing as the sons of Chinese who are American citizens and thus obtain phony passports," the article stated, adding that "many who entered this way were Red Agents."[19]

Such developments greatly altered the internal political dynamics of New York's Chinatown. Because the tense atmosphere led many Chinese to avoid involvement with leftist or progressive organizations, it gave the conservative forces in the community, particularly the KMT, an opportunity to regain their influence.

After liberation, the KMT government had retreated to Taiwan, where its existence and rule was reinforced by the presence of the U.S. military. Internationally, it continued to proclaim itself the sole "legitimate" government of the Chinese people, even though its rule covered only the Taiwanese population of 10 million. In order to give credibility to its claim, the KMT desperately needed the support—or the *illusion* of support—of overseas Chinese. In New York's Chinatown, the KMT found a willing partner in the traditional associations.

Like the KMT, the associations had suffered a decline as members were lost to the CHLA, the Seamen's Club, the Chinese Youth Club, and other independent organizations. In the 1950s, the KMT and the associations began their joint comeback by first consolidating their own alliance. The CCBA, the umbrella organization of the associations, reorganized by granting one of seven permanent positions on its executive board to the KMT. The KMT reciprocated by awarding exclusive trade privileges to "patriotic" Chinatown merchants, and by appointing prominent association leaders to the Taiwan National Assembly.

Riding the wave of anti-Communism in the United States, the KMT and the associations employed red-baiting tactics to terrorize the community into submission. They formed a Chinatown Anti-Communist League, and any group that wanted to keep out of political trouble was quick to join. The CHLA, which refused, became an outcast organization, its members harassed by the Justice Department and Immigration Office, its influence in the community all but destroyed.[20] The KMT also attacked the *China Daily News*, an independent paper with anti-KMT views, by promulgating a CCBA resolution that warned all stores and laundries "not to advertise in the *Russian Daily News [China Daily News]*.[21] The resolution was passed unanimously, and members pledged to make sure it was enforced. A number of businesses did withdraw their ads, although many complained that they had been forced into it by "certain pressures." Subscriptions were canceled by readers fearful of associating with the paper, and its circulation was soon reduced to a mere 400 subscribers.

U.S. authorities reinforced the power of the KMT and CCBA by pursuing the same targets. Most of the CHLA's leaders, for example, came under investigation on such charges as illegal entry, while the Chinese Youth Club was so constantly harassed that few dared to remain members, and by the mid-1950s it had dissolved. In March 1952, the *China Daily News* got its dose of government persecution: the paper's editor and president, Eugene Moy, was summoned with other officials to testify before the grand jury of the Southern District of New York with respect to possible violation of Title 18, No. 371, of the U.S. Code—the "Trading with the Enemy Act." The paper, it was alleged, had accepted advertising revenue from the Bank of China, the national bank of the People's Republic, while some of its staff members had sent money home to relatives (which was, as noted, a common practice). The court found the *China Daily News* guilty of the first charge; its editor was fined and its manager jailed.

The disappearance of progressive organizations in Chinatown greatly affected the daily life of the community. Working people no longer had organizations that represented and fought for their interests. The negotiating and settling of disputes, inside and outside of Chinatown, once more had to go through the autocratic and corrupt tongs and associations. Similarly, without the positive influence of the Chinese Youth Club, Chinatown's youth again resorted to gambling, drinking, and prostitution, vices found inside the tongs and associations.

By the mid-1950s, then, the "liberal" era was over in New York's Chinatown. The combined forces of U.S. conservatism and KMT reaction had put an end to free expression. Gains had been reversed and the traditional hierarchy had re-established its control: for the next two decades, the KMT and the CCBA continued to claim themselves the true representatives of the entire community.

CONCLUSION

The populations of Chinese communities in the United States tend to be viewed by outsiders as docile, apolitical, and uncommunicative. Their isolation is assumed to be self-imposed, stemming from a desire to maintain their "cultural identity." And so, to safeguard this "ethnic purity," they are believed to have reproduced traditional Chinese political and social institutions in their new communities, willingly accepting the autocratic rule of family and district associations. Chinatowns in this country, according to this stereotypic view, are static and antiquated, passed over by modern, progressive ideas, untouched by the labor movement or by class struggle.

The point of this book has been to dispel such misconceptions. First, the isolation of the Chinese was involuntary, a product of discrimination and exclusion. They have tried repeatedly to break out of this isolation, and have proved themselves active and militant opponents of racial and political oppression. Second, their acceptance of the traditional Chinese associations was not so much a matter of cultural conviction as a by-product of internal political struggle. Indeed, the history of New York's Chinatown is one of on-going class conflict between organizations representing the merchant elite and those serving the working class. Third, Chinatowns in the United States, however isolated, have scarcely been immune to changes in the larger society, both domestically and internationally—and particularly in China itself. The interconnections between political struggles within the community and those outside of it has played a major role in shaping attitudes and events in Chinatown.

I have attempted to give substance to this new and more dynamic perspective by reconstructing the history of New York's Chinatown between 1930 and 1954. Let me briefly summarize. First imported into California in the late 1840s, as a substitute for slave labor, Chinese workers were particularly important in the construction of the transcontinental railroad. But when the railroad's completion made their labor expendable, the Chinese were increasingly seen by white workers as competitors and scabs; racial attacks escalated, culminating in the prohibition of further Chinese immigration. Those who were already here were driven into urban ghettos, where the traditional merchant elite was able to impose its autocratic control over the former peasant masses.

More important, prior to the 1930s the U.S. labor movement was dominated by the craft unions, which played a leading role in the anti-Chinese agitation. Driven out of both skilled and unskilled occupations, the Chinese were left with the narrowest range of job options, and most settled in the service trades. Since they were denied access to unions, Chinese working people could not become part of the various labor struggles of the period, and this in turn prevented their full integration into the U.S. labor force.

In the 1930s, under the impact of the Great Depression, the rising militancy of the U.S. labor movement, and the progressive ideas emanating from a changing China, some sectors of New York's Chinatown attempted to break out of their isolation. A core of new and independent organizations took leadership away from the traditional associations by addressing issues of vital concern to all people in the community. By the end of the 1940s, partly as a result of the efforts of these organizations, public attitudes toward the Chinese became more favorable, allowing them a limited degree of participation in the political and economic life in the United States.

During World War II, industrial jobs at last became available to the Chinese. Moreover, while the U.S. labor movement failed to organize the majority of Chinese workers—those in the laundry and restaurant trades—it did recruit seamen into the NMU. The seamen's active participation in this union may have been the catalyst for a greater development of class consciousness throughout New York's Chinatown; it certainly represented a decided advance toward full Chinese integration into the U.S. labor movement.

Unfortunately, the political climate in the United States changed drastically in the postwar years. Influencial political figures, fearing the "communist menace," engineered a systematic purge of the U.S. left and labor movements, thus depriving the Chinese of their most sympathetic allies. At the same time, China's successful socialist revolution and involvement in the Korean war made it the arch enemy of the United States. As a result, the Chinese lost any chance of moving into the mainstream of U.S. society.

Within New York's Chinatown, too, there was regression. Riding the countrywide wave of anti-Communism, the KMT and the traditional associations employed "red-baiting" tactics to terrorize the community into submission. Progressive organizations disappeared, and with them any alternative to the autocratic and corrupt rule of the tongs and associations.

With the reemergence of the KMT and the traditional associations in the mid-1950s, Chinatown acquired a conservative, anti-Communist image in the outside world, even though its residents had fought for decades against the reactionary rule of the KMT and the traditional associations. Later on, it is true, some Chinese became increasingly ambivalent toward the new China when they realized that it was not a place where they could buy land to retire on, or as they heard reports of well-to-do relatives suffering under the revolutionary social system. The negative propaganda of the KMT and the U.S. media, of course, had its effect as well. Yet it is difficult to know what the people really felt, for the political climate in Chinatown make it impossible for anyone to voice even qualified approval of the People's Republic. For the KMT, such a silence was all it required—and desired—to successfully project its image as the "legitimate" government of the Chinese people.

NEW YORK'S CHINATOWN SINCE THE 1950s

Developments in the 1950s convinced many Chinese that while their own social mobility was limited, their children could seek a better future in the professions. Indeed, they became so committed to quality education that by 1970 the proportion of Chinese youth attending college was significantly higher than the national average. This emphasis affected the demography of the overseas Chinese communities: once the younger people gained professional skills, they moved out, leaving only the aging. In the early 1960s, sociologists like Rose Hum Lee predicted the gradual disappearance of Chinatowns as the older generation died. New York's Chinatown began to shrink, becoming a community of older first-generation males, unmarried and unaffluent. This population decline was reversed, however, with the passage of the new immigration law in 1965, which relaxed quota restrictions from Hong Kong and Taiwan.

After the gains of the 1940s, most Chinese had once again been shut out of the workforce, reinforcing a small-ownership, "petty-bourgeois" mentality and making it difficult for a working-class consciousness to develop in Chinatown. Economic and social conditions have not improved: Chinatown continues to be a highly exploited, low-wage community, with some reports indicating that the standard of living has deteriorated because of the large numbers of aging residents and of newly arrived immigrants without "marketable skills" or a command of the English language. Appeals based on a working-class ideology have proved ineffective, and attempts by young militants in the early 1970s to mobilize the community on the basis of class solidarity and unity with other "oppressed" Third World minorities met with the same difficulties the Chinese left had faced in the 1930s.

Prospects for the future development of a working-class consciousness are more promising. The availability of cheap labor has drawn many investors to Chinatown in recent years, spawning garment factories, restaurants, and other labor-intensive industries and leading to a rapid proletarianization of the community's working people. Because of their low wages and harsh conditions, these have remained exclusively Chinese trades. For the hundreds of workers employed in these operations, traditional family, clan, and regional ties have been weakened and class divisions intensified. Labor organizations have grown: an increasing number of Chinese belong to the International Ladies' Garment Workers' Union, all the workers in the larger restaurants outside Chinatown have been unionized, and there are signs of mobilization among restaurant workers inside the community as well. But while the conditions of Chinese in the United States have improved, it is the middle, professional classes living outside of Chinatown whose conditions have improved the most. Chinatowns remain urban ghettos: the crowded living quarters are deteriorating rapidly, health care facilities are lacking, and the educational system is inferior. Patriotism remains the most important factor in the political consciousness of New York's Chinese. Patriotic activities, as we have seen, have been the only concrete way for Chinese in the United States to react to discrimination, to reach out for the support and acceptance of U.S. society as a whole. As long as they continue to experience discrimination, they will tend to look to China as a source of relief, even if it be only emotional or psychological. Thousands of Chinese go to every showing of a movie or troupe from the mainland, even if it is way outside of Chinatown. There are ten Chinese-language dailies, only one among them clearly pro-Peking, the others anti-Communist or "neutral," but all giving prominent and detailed coverage to events in China. This clearly reflects the newspapers' attempt to satisfy the interests of the community.

This abiding concern with the homeland has put the Chinese in a contradictory position, for the sharp differences between the social and political systems of China and the United States are not overcome by the present warming of the relationship between the two. And while there is a great enthusiasm in the community for improved relations, expressions of patriotism have so far been cautious, particularly among those who lived through the 1950s. Certainly, those who push for social change in the community will have to be concerned about being castigated for their "pro-Communism," much as the radicals of the 1930s were.

As far as Chinatown's political structure is concerned, there are drastic changes in the making. The power bases of the CCBA and the traditional associations—the KMT and the Nationalist government on the one hand, and the local merchant elite on the other—are in rapid decline. As relations between China and the United States have become friendly, the KMT has lost its position of influence in the community. At the same time, the recent wave of liberation struggles in the Far East has led many large Chinese business interests in those areas to emigrate to New York, creating financial blocs that have overwhelmed the old merchant elite. There has been an economic boom in New York's Chinatown, with the new interests swallowing up larger and larger sections of its business district. This shift in the economic balance of power has demanded a different political structure, and the present instability in the community—especially the persistent gang wars of recent years—is the result of a struggle for ascendancy among competing financial interests.

There are other challengers to the old political structure. Local, state, and city social welfare agencies have become an important force in the past few years as Chinatown (now recognized as a minority poverty area) has received public assistance in the form of old-age assistance, youth education, drug prevention programs, and job training for new immigrants. Many Chinese are developing political contacts with the government in order to maintain and increase these benefits, and are thus becoming involved in local party politics. Some are beginning to develop Chinese voting blocs to assist in their bid for power. Chinatown's Republican and Democratic party branches are growing, the Democratic Party particularly, because of its more liberal outlook on social and welfare issues. As political power in Chinatown becomes a matter of a candidate's "voter appeal" and capacity to deliver social benefits to the community, the traditional systems of hierarchical authority should become less and less relevant.

BEYOND THE MELTING POT

I felt that a study of New York's Chinatown such as this was necessary because the particular experiences of the Chinese are not fully explained by the current literature on the integration of minorities in this country. Clearly, the treatment of the Chinese speaks against the validity of the already battered "melting-pot" theory, whereby new immigrants are incorporated into U.S. society gradually, and full integration is only a matter of time. The Chinese have been in this country for over a hundred years, and large numbers of them are still living in poverty-stricken ghettos. They are not "exceptions."

Such contradictory evidence has led some scholars to revise the melting-pot theory, claiming that it is not applicable to the "colored" minorities because "racism" is the one factor that resists the "melting" process. Yet while the concept of "racism" is in wide use today, it by no means explains everything—least of all why its effect on the Chinese was not identical to its effect on other "colored" minorities. A "national" approach, as I have tried to demonstrate, provides a far more satisfactory account of the Chinese experience in this country.

Another weakness in the existing scholarship on "ethnic studies" is the lack of a systematic and specific class focus in the analysis of immigrant groups. These studies tend to regard admission into elite professional areas as the primary index of the well-being of a particular minority group. Yet new arrivals often have to seek low-level jobs, for instance, as manual workers. For the majority, acceptance into the wage-labor force, not the professional elite, is the most important indicator of "advancement." A negative response from the trade unions will force a group to continue to work in the low-paid, first-fired–last-hired categories. The few individuals who have been accepted into the middle-class professions will have no effect on the majority, who continue to experience the oppression of discrimination. Upward mobility will be blocked unless the newly arrived immigrants are able to pursue advancement into a nonworker category, generally as small self-employed businessmen.

For the Chinese, the craft-union's anti-Chinese stance precluded their integration into the U.S. working class, forcing them into self-employed service trades and, in the long run, confirming their isolation. Yet the Chinese want to join unions; in 1974, during the construction of a large housing project in New York's China-town, workers with the requisite skills demonstrated at the job site, demanding employment from management and the building-trades union.

A systematic focus on the choices available to a minority group helps explain the reasons behind its "ethnic professional preference." The fact that many Jews and Chinese seek jobs in small businesses and are thought to be "tightfisted" can thus be explained; there is a certain logic, too, to the fact that large numbers of Koreans operate vegetable stands and Greeks run lunch counters.

One last criticism of the current literature on "integration" is its overt reliance on "culture" and "values" to explain minority behavior. The assumption is that the social and political conditions of a particular immigrant community reflect a voluntary commitment to certain cultural traditions and values. The reasoning, however, is circular. The real question is why some groups cling tightly to their "traditional" heritage while others discard it rapidly. In the final analysis, survival, not cultural preservation, is the primary objective of most immigrant groups. The tenacity of a cultural tradition may represent nothing more than a closing of ranks in response to the rejection of a group's attempts to open outward.

When the Chinese were forced into isolation, for example, they defended themselves by erecting strong, traditional institutions; they did not create this "cultural enclave" out of choice.

There is a related tendency in integration-oriented studies to take the existing superstructure of a minority community as "given," as automatically reflecting the preferred values and ideology of the majority of its inhabitants. Yet the shape of the superstructure may in part be determined by the subjective preferences—and calculated intervention—of U.S. society. It is not unknown, after all, for U.S. authorities to step into political struggles within minority communities in order to ensure the victory of whatever side is ideologically compatible with "mainstream values." Sometimes this is done indirectly, by sanctioning the intervention of home governments in such struggles, ultimately against the interests and wishes of the community. In the 1950s, the U.S. government's "anti-Communist" stance in support of the KMT and the Nationalist government certainly prolonged the survival of a corrupt and impotent—but ideologically acceptable—superstructure in Chinatown. What is worse, by helping the KMT eliminate its political opponents, the U.S. government also hastened the destruction of progressive forces in the community that could have led the Chinese toward fuller integration into the labor force.

The Chinese case is not unique; a pervasive ignorance of the internal dynamics of minority groups too often leads the U.S. public to tolerate these tactics. Today, many minority communities are voicing fears about the repressive operations of their home governments in the United States. Koreans, for instance, have complained for years about Park Chung Hee's secret police intimidating their nationals. Haitians and Filipinos are constantly aware of the intimidation of the so-called "extreme right" in their communities in the United States, which make their freedom of expression difficult. These complaints must not be reduced to the status of mere squabbles between the home governments and their overseas nationals: they are symptomatic of the U.S. government's approach to certain nationality groupings in this country.

NOTES

CHAPTER 1: NEW YORK'S CHINATOWN BEFORE 1930

1. Harley MacNair, *The Chinese Abroad* (Shanghai: Commercial Press, 1924), p. 2, and Sun Wa-tao, *Mei-kuo hua-ch'aio shih-lu* [History of Chinese in America] (Taipei: 1962), p. 1.
2. *Hua-ch'aio chih chung-chih* [Summary History of Chinese Overseas] (Taipei: Hai Wai Publishing Co., 1956), pp. 94–95.
3. MacNair, *The Chinese Abroad*, p. 210.
4. Gunther Barth, *Bitter Strength: A History of the Chinese in the United States, 1850–1870* (Cambridge, Mass.: Harvard University Press, 1964).
5. H. M. Lai and P. P. Choy, *Outline History of the Chinese in America* (San Francisco: 1972), p. 40.
6. Stuart Creighton Miller, *The Unwelcomed Immigrant: American Image of the Chinese, 1785–1882* (Berkeley: University of California Press, 1969), p. 36.
7. Elmer Clarence Sandmeyer, *The Anti-Chinese Movement in California* (Chicago: University of Illinois Press, 1973), p. 26.
8. James W. Loewen, *The Mississippi Chinese: Between Black and White* (Cambridge, Mass.: Harvard University Press, 1971), pp. 22–23.
9. Alexander Saxton, *The Indispensible Enemy: Labor and the Anti-Chinese Movement in California* (Berkeley: University of California Press, 1971), p. 57.
10. George F. Seward, *Chinese Immigration in Its Social and Economic Aspects* (New York: Charles Scribner's, 1881), p. 43.
11. Carey McWilliams, *Factories in the Field* (Santa Barbara: Peregrine Publishers, 1971), pp. 70–73.
12. Saxton, *The Indispensible Enemy*, p. 11.
13. Thomas W. Chin, ed., *A History of Chinese in California: A Syllabus* (San

Francisco: Chinese Historical Society of America, 1969), p. 24.

14. Kate Holladay Claghorn, *The Immigrant's Day in Court* (New York: Arno Press, 1969), p. 306.

15. Mary Robert Coolidge, *Chinese Immigration* (New York: Henry Holt and Co., 1909), p. 75.

16. Ibid., p. 76.

17. Paul Jacobs and Saul Landau, *They Serve the Devil* (New York: Vintage Books, 1971), p. 104.

18. Isabella Black, "American Labor and Chinese Immigration," *Past and Present* 25 (1964): 67.

19. Saxton, *The Indispensible Enemy*, p. 75.

20. Herbert Hill, "Anti-Oriental Agitation and the Rise of Working-Class Racism," *Society* (January–February 1973): 47.

21. Black, "American Labor and Chinese Immigration," p. 64.

22. Ibid., p. 67.

23. Saxton, *The Indispensible Enemy*, p. 271.

24. Black, "American Labor and Chinese Immigration," p. 69.

25. Saxton, *The Indispensible Enemy*, p. 273.

26. William Preston, Jr., *Aliens and Dissenters* (Cambridge, Mass.: Harvard University Press, 1963).

27. Shen I-yao, *Hai-wai p'ai-hua pai-nien shih* [Hundred Year History of Anti-Chinese Movements] (Hong Kong: Wan Yu Press, 1970), pp. 12–13.

28. Cheng Tsu Wu, "Chinese People and Chinatown in New York City," Ph.D. diss., Clark University, 1958, p. 12, and David Te-chao Cheng, "Acculturation of the Chinese in the United States," Ph.D. diss., University of Pennsylvania, 1948, p. 54

29. Stanford M. Lyman, *Chinese Americans* (New York: Random House, 1974), p. 86.

30. Eng Ying Gong and Bruce Grant, *Tong War!* (New York: Nicholas L. Brown, 1930), p. 286.

CHAPTER 2: POLITICAL AND LABOR MOVEMENTS

1. Lawrence K. Rosinger, *China's Wartime Politics: 1937–1944* (Princeton: Princeton University Press, 1945), p. 9.

2. Interviews with old time resident of New York's Chinatown, Case #1, and H. M. Lai, "A Historical Survey of Organization of the Left Among the Chinese in America," *Bulletin of Concerned Asian Scholars* 4, no. 3 (Fall 1972): 12.

3. Mei Li Tsuan, "Mei-kuo hua-jen tso-pei yün-tung chein-shih," [Short History of Chinese American Left Movement], *Wei Min Asian American News*, June 1973, p. 8.

4. *Chinese Nationalist Daily [Min-ch'i jih-pao]*, August 16, 1933, p. 10.

5. *Chinese Vanguard [Hsien-fung pao]*, March 1, 1933, p. 3.

6. *The Communist*, July 1934, p. 703.

7. *Chinese Vanguard*, September 15, 1932, p. 3.

8. Ibid., February 1, 1933, p. 1.

9. Ibid., February 15, 1933, p. 4.

10. Chu Y. K., *Mei-kuo hua-ch'iao kai-shih* [History of the Chinese People in America] (New York: China Times Press, 1975), pp. 112–114.

11. *Chinese Nationalist Daily*, January 29, 1933, p. 3, and Gor Yun Leong, *Chinatown Inside Out* (New York: Barrows Mussey, 1936), p. 51.

12. Frances F. Piven and Richard A. Cloward, *Regulating the Poor* (New York: Vintage Books, 1971), p. 105, and *Labor Unity* (New York), August 22, 1931, p. 8.

13. *Chinese Nationalist Daily*, January 11, 1933, p. 7.

14. Ibid., January 17, 1933, p. 7.

15. Leong, *Chinatown Inside Out*, p. 51, *Daily Worker*, March 14, 1933, p. 2, and *Chinese Vanguard*, March 15, 1933, p. 3.

16. *Chinese Nationalist Daily*, January 16, 1934, p. 9.

17. *Daily Worker*, various issues in April 1933.

18. Betty Lee Sung, *Mountain of Gold* (New York: MacMillan, 1967), p. 188, Wu, "Chinese People and Chinatown," p. 32, and Leong, *Chinatown Inside Out*, p. 36.

19. Paul C. P. Siu, "The Chinese Laundrymen: A Study of Social Isolation," Ph.D. diss., University of Chicago, 1953, p. 166.

20. *Progressive Laundryman*, April, 1932, p. 19.

21. Leong, *Chinatown Inside Out*, p. 33.

22. *Nationalist Daily*, April 24, 1933, p. 4.

23. Ibid., April 27, 1933, p. 9.

24. Virginia Heyer, "Pattern of Social Organization in New York City's Chinatown," Ph.D. diss., Columbia University, 1953, p. 93.

CHAPTER 3: OLD AGAINST NEW

1. *Nationalist Daily*, May 5, 1933, p. 9.

2. Ibid., June 28, 29, 30, 1933.

3. Leong, *Chinatown Inside Out*, Introduction.

4. *Chinese Nationalist Daily*, July 11, 1933, p. 10.

5. Edward Corsi, *In the Shadow of Liberty* (New York: Arno Press, 1969), p. 169.

6. *Chinese Vanguard*, April 15, 1934, p. 1.

7. Ibid., March 11, 1935, p. 3.

8. Mei Li Tsuan, "Mei-kuo hua-jen," p. 12.

9. Ibid.

10. Leong, *Chinatown Inside Out*, p. 102, and *Nationalist Daily*, March 17, 1934, p. 9.

11. *Chinese Nationalist Daily*, May 11, 1934, p. 9, and May 19, 28, 1934.

12. Mei Li Tsuan, "Mei-kuo hua-jen," p. 12.

13. Shepherd Schwartz, "The Chinese Community in New York City," CURCC, unpublished documents, 1950, p. 40, *China Daily News [Hua-chao jih-pao]*, May 26, 1941, p. 6, and *Hua-ch'iao chin-nien chiu-kuo tuan te-k'an* [Chinese Youth Club Annual Issue], nos. 1, 2, 3.

14. *Chinese Vanguard*, April 28, 1938, p. 3.

15. *Fraternal Order* (New York: International Workers' Order), vol. 1, no. 5 (1939): 11, and vol. 7, nos. 8–9 (1945).

16. Walter Galenson, *The CIO Challenge to the AFL: A History of the American Labor Movement, 1935–1941* (Cambridge, Mass.: Harvard University Press, 1960), p. 287.

17. Ivan Light, *Ethnic Enterprise in America: Business and Welfare Among Chinese, Japanese, and Blacks* (Berkeley: University of California Press, 1972), p. 93.

18. William Z. Foster, *American Trade Unionism* (New York: International Publishers, 1954), p. 196, and *Labor Fact Book II* (New York: International Publishers, Labor Research Association, 1934), p. 117.

19. Leong, *Chinatown Inside Out*, p. 101.

20. *Chinese Vanguard*, March 23, 1935, p. 3.

21. Ibid., October 5, 1935, p. 1.

22. *Chinese Nationalist Daily*, October 16, 1939, p. 3.

23. *China Daily News*, October 22, 1940, p. 7.

24. *Chinese Nationalist Daily*, May 26, 1939, p. 3.

25. Ibid., April 24, 1939, p. 8, and *China Salvation Times [Chiu-kuo shih-pao]*, April 20, 1939, p. 3.

CHAPTER 4: THE PATRIOTIC MOVEMENTS

1. Lai and Choy, *Outline History of the Chinese in America*, p. 136.
2. Roger Daniels, *The Politics of Prejudice* (New York: Atheneum, 1970), p. 36.
3. Ibid., p. 35.
4. *New York hua-ch'iao chu-jih hou-yuan-hui cheng-hsing-lou* [New York Chinese Anti-Japanese Support Committee Bulletin] (New York: Nationalist Daily Publications, 1929), p. 141.
5. Chu Sha, "Mei-hua ch'iao-yu ch'iao-tuan" [Overseas Chinese and Overseas Organizations], *China Post* (New York), September 16, 1972, p. 9.
6. Ibid., September 18, 1972.
7. *New York Hua-ch'iao fu-nü ai-kuo hui wu-chou-nien* [Chinese Women's Association Fifth Anniversary Special Issue], pp. 52–55.
8. *Chinese Vanguard*, September 1, 1934, p. 1.
9. Tsai Ting-kai, *Hai-wai ying-hsiang chi* [Impressions from Overseas Travels] (Hong Kong: Publications Limited, 1935), and Chu Sha, in *China Post*, September 25, 1972, p. 9.
10. *China Post*, September 26, 1972.
11. Tomohide Normura, "Some Aspects of the United Front in China," Masters essay, Columbia University, 1961, p. 30.
12. *Chinese Vanguard*, September 28, 1935, p. 3.
13. Ibid., December 7, 1935, p. 1.
14. Ibid., December 21, 1935, p. 1, and Lyman, *Chinese Americans*, p. 33.
15. *Chinese Vanguard*, December 28, 1935, and January 4, 1936, p. 1.
16. *Chinese Nationalist Daily*, June 19, 1936, p. 9.
17. *Liu-mei hsieh-sheng yueh-k'an* [Chinese Student Monthly], March 1937.
18. *China Daily News*, July 8, 1940, p. 7.
19. George Seldes, *Facts and Fascism* (New York: In Fact, Inc., 1943), pp. 40–50.
20. *Chinese Vanguard*, October 14, 1937, p. 2.
21. *China Salvation Times*, May 18, 1939, p. 4.
22. *I-lien wu-chou-nien te-k'an* [Chinese Hand Laundry Alliance Fifth Anniversary Special Bulletin], p. 51.
23. Harold R. Isaacs, *Scratches on Our Minds* (New York: John Day, 1958), p. 71.
24. *Liu-mei hsieh-sheng yueh-k'an* [Chinese Student Monthly], April 1936, p. 15, and August 1936, p. 4.
25. *The NMU Fights Jim Crow* (a NMU official publication), pp. 5–6.
26. *Shanghai Evening Post and Mercury* (New York), March 26, 1943, p. 3.

CHAPTER 5: PIONEERS IN INTEGRATION

1. Chuan-hua Lowe, *Facing Labor Issues in China* (Shanghai: China Institute of Pacific Relations, 1933), p. 52.
2. Jean Chesneaux, *The Chinese Labor Movement, 1919–1927* (Stanford: Stanford University Press, 1968), p. 298.
3. *Daily Worker*, March 1, 1933, p. 4.
4. *Chinese Vanguard*, February 1, 1933, p. 1.
5. Hugh Mulzac, *A Star to Steer By* (New York: International Publishers, 1963), pp. 112–114, and Richard O. Boyer, *The Dark Ship* (Boston: Little Brown and Co., 1947), p. 114.
6. Mulzac, *A Star to Steer By*, p. 123.
7. Donald T. Critchow, "Communist Unions and Racism: A Comparative Study," *Labor History* 17, no. 2 (Spring 1976): 237, and *Steering to Victory*, a NMU pamphlet.
8. *Chinese Nationalist Daily*, November 17, 1936, p. 3.
9. S. S. Tow, *Mei-kuo tai-yü hua-ch'iao lü-lich chieh-yao* [Digest of Laws, Rules and Court Decisions Governing the Chinese in America] (New York: Hua Chao Publications, 1928), pp. 12–13, and *Chinese Vanguard*, June 26, 1937, p. 2.
10. *Chinese Vanguard*, June 26, 1937, p. 2.
11. Boyer, *The Dark Ship*, p. 100.
12. *Enemy at Home*, a NMU pamphlet, p. 194.
13. *China Daily News*, November 11, 1942, p. 7.
14. Ibid., August 3, 1942, p. 7.
15. *Shanghai Evening Post and Mercury*, June 7, 1943, p. 4.
16. *China Daily News*, April 3, 1943, p. 2.
17. Ibid., December 20, 22, 1942, and January 6, 1943.
18. *Shanghai Evening Post and Mercury*, June 14, 1943, p. 6.
19. *China Daily News*, January 25, 1943, p. 6.
20. *China Daily News*, February 17 and March 15, 1943.
21. Ibid., August 10 and 11, 1943, p. 6.
22. Ibid., August 18, 1945, p. 7.

CHAPTER 6: THE CHINESE REVOLUTION

1. *China Daily News*, February 10, 1943, p. 2.
2. Ibid., November 17, 1943, p. 7.
3. *Hsin Pao*, July 13, 1945, p. 8.

4. Ibid., February 17, 1944, p. 1.
5. *China Daily News*, August 14, 1945, p. 7.
6. *Hsin Pao*, June 19, 1945, p. 8.
7. Edmund O. Clubb, *Twentieth Century China* (New York: Columbia University Press, 1964), p. 260, and Herbert Feis, *The China Tangle* (Princeton: Princeton University Press, 1953), pp. 364–366.
8. Clubb, *Twentieth Century China*, p. 291, and Chu Y. K., *Mei-kuo hua*, p. 140.
9. Barnett, *China on the Eve of Communist Takeover*, p. 97.
10. *Hsin Pao*, August 19, 1946, p. 8.
11. *China Daily News*, December 20, 22, 1948, and January 26, 1949, p. 7.
12. Albert Kahn, *High Treason* (New York: Lear Publishers, 1950), p. 268.
13. *China Daily News*, November 18, 1946, p. 2.
14. Kahn, *High Treason*, p. 284.
15. Ibid., p. 308.
16. *China Daily News*, April 4, 1946, p. 3.
17. Interview with Kwong's lawyer.
18. *Chinese Students in the United States, 1948–1955* (New York: Committee on Educational Interchange Policy, March 1956).
19. *U.S. News and World Report*, April 20, 1956.
20. Virginia Heyer "Pattern of Social Organization in New York City's Chinatown," Ph.D. diss., Columbia University, 1933, p. 94.
21. *The Facts Behind the China Daily News Case* (New York: The Committee to Support the China Daily News, 1955), pp. 10–11.

BIBLIOGRAPHY

BIBLIOGRAPHY OF PRIMARY SOURCES

1. Chinese-language newspapers

China Daily News [Hua-ch'iao jih-pao], New York City, 1940 to 1955.
China Salvation Times [Chiu-kuo shih-pao], New York City, 1938 to 1939.
China Times [Chung-kuo jih-pao], New York City, 1972 to 1973.
Chinese Nationalist Daily [Min-ch'i jih-pao], New York City, 1929 to 1948.
Chinese Vanguard [Hsien-fung pao], New York City, 1930 to 1937.
Golden Gate Chinese Times [Chin-shan jih-pao], San Francisco, 1945 to 1947.
Hsin Pao, New York City, 1946 to 1948.
Wei Min Asian American News [Wei-min pao], San Francisco, 1972 to 1974.

2. Chinese-language books

Chang Ts'un-wu. *Kuang-hsü shan-shih-i-nien chung-mei kung-yüeh fung-tsao*
    [1904 Chinese Boycott of American Goods in Protest of American Treat-
    ment of Overseas Chinese]. Taipai: Central Government Research Division
    Publications.
Ch'en Li-te. *Chung-kuo hai-wai i-min shih* [History of Chinese Emigration].
    Shanghai: China Books and Publications, 1946.
Chu Shih-chia. *Mei-kuo pi-hai hua-ch'iao shih-liao* [Historical Material on
    American Oppression Against Chinese Labor]. Peking: 1958.
Chu Y. K. *Mei-kuo hua-ch'iao kai-shih* [History of the Chinese People in America].
    New York: China Times Press, 1975.
Feng Chih-yu. *Hua-ch'iao k'e-ming shih-hua* [Revolutionary Heritage of the
    Overseas Chinese]. Chungking: Hai Wai Publishing Co., 1945.
Hua-ch'iao chih chung-chih [Summary History of Chinese Overseas]. Taipei: Hai
    Wai Publishing Co., 1956.

Huang Chen-wu. *Hua-ch'iao yü chung-kuo ke-ming* [Overseas Chinese and Chinese Revolutions]. Taipei: Research Division of the Defense Department, 1963.

Ku Kün. *Chung-kuo ching-tai-shih shang ti pu-ping-teng tiao-yüeh* [Recent History of Unequal Treaties Against China]. Hong Kong: Tsao Yung Publishing Co., 1975.

Lee Ch'ang-fu. *Chung-kuo i-min shih* [Chinese Emigration History]. Taipei: Taiwan Commercial Press, 1966.

Liu shih-mu. *Hua-ch'iao kai-kuan* [A General View of Overseas Chinese]. Shanghai: China Books and Publications, 1935.

Liu Ta-nien. *Mei-kuo ching hua chien-shih* [Short History of American Aggression Against China]. Peking: New China Publications, 1950.

Shen I-yao. *Ha-wai p'ai-hua pai-nien shih* [Hundred-Year History of Anti-Chinese Movements]. Hong Kong: Wan Yu Publication Co., 1970.

Shuai Hsueh-fu. *Chung-kuo pang-hui shih* [History of Chinese Secret Societies]. Hong Kong: Modern Publications, 1960.

Sun Wa-tao. *Mei-kuo hua-ch'iao shih-lu* [History of Chinese in America]. Taipei: 1962.

Ting Tse-min. *Mei-kuo p'ai-hua shih* [American Anti-Chinese Movements]. Shanghai: China Publications, 1952.

Tow, S. S. *Mei-kuo tai-yü hua-ch'iao lü-lieh chieh-yao* [Digest of Laws, Rules and Court Decisions Governing the Chinese in America]. New York: Hua Chao Publications, 1928.

Tsai Ting-kai. *Hai-wai ying-hsiang chi* [Impressions from Overseas Travels]. Hong Kong: Publications Limited, 1935.

Wu Shang-yin. *Mei-kuo hua-ch'iao pai-nien chi-shih* [Hundred Year History of Chinese in America]. Hong Kong: 1954.

Young Kang. *Mei-kuo cha chi* [Miscellaneous Memories of the United States of America]. Peking: World Publications, 1951.

3. *Chinese-language periodicals and pamphlets*

I-lien wu-chou-nien te k'an [Chinese Hand Laundry Alliance Fifth Anniversary Special Bulletin]. New York: 1938.

Liu-mei hsieh-sheng yueh k'an [Chinese Student Monthly]. Chicago: The Chinese Student Association of North America, 1934–1938.

New York hua-ch'iao fu-nü ai-kuo hui wu-chou-nien [New York Chinese Women's Association Fifth Anniversary Special Issue]. New York: Chinese Women's Association, Inc., 1936.

Hua-ch'iao chin-nien chiu-kuo tuan te-k'an [Chinese Youth Club Annual Issues #1, 2, 3]. New York Chinese Patriotic Youth Club, 1939, 1940, 1941.

Shih-yeh kung-jen yueh-k'an [Chinese Unemployed Workers' Monthly]. New York Chinese Unemployed Council Publication, 1933.

New York hua-ch'iao chu-jih hou-yuan-hui cheng-hsing-lou [New York Chinese Anti-Japanese Support Committee Bulletin]. New York: Nationalist Daily Publications, 1929.

4. English-language periodicals and pamphlets

Chinese Students in the United States, 1948–1955. New York: Committee on Education Interchange Policy, March 1956.

Chinatown 1969. New York: Chinatown '69 Research Group.

China Today. New York: Friends of China. (A monthly magazine of information and opinion, from 1934–1941.)

The Communist (journal). Communist Party, U.S.A., from 1933–1940.

The Daily Worker (newspaper). Communist Party, U.S.A., from 1929–1940.

The Facts Behind the China Daily News Case. New York: Committee to Support the China Daily News, 1955.

Fraternal Order (periodical). New York: International Workers' Order, 1938–1945.

Labor Fact Books II to X. New York: International Publishers, Labor Research Association, 1934–.

Labor History. New York: Tamiment Institute of Labor Studies, New York University, 1972–.

The Pilot. New York: NMU, 1937–.

Progressive Laundryman. New York: American Laundryman Association, 1932–1940.

The Shanghai Evening Post and Mercury. New York: 1943–1946.

BIBLIOGRAPHY OF SECONDARY SOURCES

An Outline History of China. Peking: Foreign Language Press, [1958].

Austin, Alline. *The Labor Story: A Popular History of American Labor, 1786–1949.* New York: Coward-McCann Inc., 1949.

Barnett, A. Doak. *China on the Eve of Communist Takeover.* New York: Frederick A. Praeger, 1968.

Barth, Gunther. *Bitter Strength: A History of the Chinese in the United States, 1850–1870.* Cambridge, Mass.: Harvard University Press, 1964.

Beck, Louis J. *New York's Chinatown.* New York: Bohemia Publishing Co., 1898.

Biano, Lucian. *Origins of the Chinese Revolution 1915–1949*. London: Oxford University Press, 1970.

Boyer, Richard O. *The Dark Ship*. Boston: Little Brown and Co., 1947.

Boyer, Richard O. and Morais, Herbert M. *Labor's Untold Story*. New York: United Electrical Workers, 1955.

Campbell, Persia Cramford. *The Chinese Coolie Emigration*. London: P. S. King and Son Ltd., 1923.

Cattell, Stuart H. *Health, Welfare, and Social Organization in Chinatown, New York City*. New York: Community Service Society of New York, August 1962.

Chang, Hsin-pao. *Commissioner Lim and the Opium War*. New York: W. W. Norton, 1964.

Cheng, David Te-chao. "Acculturation of the Chinese in the United States, A Philadelphia Study." Ph.D. diss., University of Pennsylvania, 1948.

Cheng, Tien-fong. *A History of Sino-Russian Relations*. Washington: Public Affairs Press, 1957.

Chesneaux, Jean. *The Chinese Labor Movement, 1919–1927*. Stanford: Stanford University Press, 1968.

Chinese Working People in America: A Pictorial History. San Francisco: Wei Min She' Labor Committee, United Front Press, 1974.

Chin, Thomas W., ed. *A History of the Chinese in California: A Syllabus*. San Francisco: Chinese Historical Society of America, 1969.

Chiu, Ping. *Chinese Labor in California: An Economic Study*. Madison: Department of History, University of Wisconsin, 1963.

Claghorn, Kate Holladay. *The Immigrant's Day in Court*. New York: Arno Press, 1969.

Clubb, Edmund O. *Twentieth Century China*. New York: Columbia University Press, 1964.

Coleman, Elizabeth. *Chinatown U.S.A., Texts and Photographs*. New York: John Day Co., 1946.

Compton, Boyd. *Mao's China: Party Reform Documents, 1942–1944*. Seattle: University of Washington Press, 1952.

Coolidge, Mary Robert. *Chinese Immigration*. New York: Henry Holt and Co., 1909.

Corsi, Edward. *In the Shadow of Liberty*. New York: Arno Press, 1969.

Daniels, Roger. *The Politics of Prejudice*. New York: Atheneum Press, 1970.

Dillon, Richard H. *The Hatchet Man*. New York: Coward-McCann, 1962.

Fairbank, John King. *The United States and China*. New York: The Viking Press, 1967.

Feis, Herbert. *The China Tangle*. Princeton: Princeton University Press, 1953.

Feldman, H. *Racial Factors in American Industry*. New York: Harper and Brothers, 1931.

Fitzgerald, Stephen. *China and the Overseas Chinese: A Study of Peking's Changing Policy, 1949–1970*. London: Cambridge University Press, 1972.

Fong, Ng Bickleen. *The Chinese in New Zealand*. Hong Kong: Hong Kong University Press, 1957.

Foster, William Z. *American Trade Unionism*. New York: International Publishers, 1954.

——— *The Negro People*. New York: International Publishers, 1954.

Franklin, Charles Lionel. *The Negro Labor Unionist of New York*. New York: AMS Press, 1968.

Fried, Morton H., ed. *Colloquim on Overseas Chinese*. New York: Institute of Pacific Relations, 1958.

Galenson, Walter. *The CIO Challenge to the AFL: A History of the American Labor Movement, 1935–1941*. Cambridge, Mass.: Harvard University Press, 1960.

Glazer, Nathan and Moynihan, Daniel Patrick, eds. *Beyond the Melting Pot*. Boston: M.I.T. Press, 1963.

Glick, Carl. *Shake Hands with the Dragon*. New York: Whittlesay House, 1941.

Gong, Eng Ying and Grant, Bruce. *Tong War!* New York: Nicholas L. Brown, 1930.

Gray, Jack. *Modern China's Search for a Political Form*. London: Oxford University Press, 1969.

Green, Philip and Levison, Sanford, eds. *Power and Community: Dissenting Essays in Political Science*. New York: Vintage Books, 1970.

Gutman, Herbert G. *Work, Culture, and Society in Industrializing America*. New York: Alfred A. Knopf, 1976.

Hawkins, Brett W. and Lorinkas, Robert A., eds. *The Ethnic Factor in American Politics*. Columbus: Charles E. Merrill Pub. Co., 1970.

Heyer, Virginia. "Pattern of Social Organization in New York City's Chinatown." Ph.D. diss., Columbia University, 1953.

Hoy, William. *The Six Companies*. San Francisco: CCBA, 1942.

Hsiong, George L., ed. *Chinatown and Her Mother Country*. Shanghai: New China Co., 1939.

Isaacs, Harold R. *Scratches on Our Minds*. New York: John Day, 1958.

Jacobs, Paul and Landau, Saul. *They Serve the Devil*. New York: Vintage Books, 1971.

Johnson, Chalmers A. *Peasant Nationalism and Communist Power*. Stanford: Stanford University Press, 1962.

Kahn, Albert. *High Treason*. New York: Lear Publishers, 1950.

Koen, Ross Y. *The China Lobby in American Politics*. New York: Harper and Row, 1974.

Konvitz, Milton R. *The Alien and the Asiatic in American Law*. Ithaca: Cornell University Press, 1953.

Kung, S. W. *Chinese in American Life: Some Aspects of Their History, Status, Problems, and Contributions*. Seattle: University of Washington Press, 1962.

Lai, H. M. and Choy, P. P. *Outline History of the Chinese in America*. San Francisco: 1972.

Lane, Robert E. *Political Life*. New York: The Free Press, 1959.

Lee, Calvin. *Chinatown, U.S.A.* New York: Doubleday, 1965.

Lee, Rose Hum. *The Chinese in the United States of America*. Hong Kong: Hong Kong University Press, 1960.

Lenin, V. I. *Lenin on the National and Colonial Questions: Three Articles*. Peking: Foreign Language Press, 1970.

Leong, Gor Yun. *Chinatown Inside Out*. New York: Barrows Mussey, 1936.

Light, Ivan. *Ethnic Enterprise in America: Business and Welfare Among Chinese, Japanese, and Blacks*. Berkeley: University of California Press, 1972.

Loewen, James W. *The Mississippi Chinese: Between Black and White*. Cambridge, Mass.: Harvard University Press, 1971.

Lorigan, Edna. *Unemployed in N.Y.C.* New York: Welfare Council of N.Y.C., 1931.

Lowe, Chuan-hua. *Facing Labor Issues in China*. Shanghai: China Institute of Pacific Relations, 1933.

Lyman, Stanford M. *The Asian in the West*. Reno: Social Science and Humanities Publications, 1970.

————. *Chinese Americans*. New York: Random House, 1974.

McClellan, Robert. *The Heathen Chinese: A Study of American Attitudes Toward China, 1890–1905*. Columbus: Ohio State University Press, 1971.

MacNair, Harley F. *The Chinese Abroad*. Shanghai: Commercial Press, 1924.

McWilliams, Carey. *Brothers Under the Skin*. Boston: Little, Brown and Co., 1964.

————. *Factories in the Field*. Santa Barbara: Peregrine Publishers, 1971.

Mao Tse-tung. *Selected Works of Mao Tse-tung*. Peking: Foreign Language Press, 1970.

Marshall, Ray. *The Negro Worker*. New York: Random House, 1967.

Miller, Stuart Creighton. *The Unwelcome Immigrant: American Image of the Chinese, 1785–1882*. Berkeley: University of California Press, 1969.

Mulzac, Hugh. *A Star to Steer By*. New York: International Publishers, 1963.

National Maritime Union (NMU), selected pamphlets:
    The NMU Fights Jim Crow

Steering to Victory
Enemy at Home

Nee, Victor and Brett. *Long Time Californ'*. New York: Random House, 1972.

Nestel, Louis Paul. *Labor Relations in the Laundry Industry in Greater N.Y.* New York: 1950.

Nomura, Tomohide. "Some Aspects of the United Front in China." Masters essay, Columbia University, 1961.

North, Robert C. *Moscow and Chinese Communists*. Stanford: Stanford University Press, 1965.

Ohomki, Emiko. "The Detroit Chinese: A Study of Social Cultural Changes in the Detroit Chinese Community." Masters essay, University of Wisconsin.

Overseas Chinese Rally to the Aid the Fatherland. Shanghai: The Federation of Chinese Cultural Associations, 1938.

Park, No-yong. *Chinaman's Chance*. Boston: Meadow Publishing Co., 1940.

Piven, Frances Fox and Cloward, Richard A. *Regulating the Poor*. New York: Vintage Books, 1971.

Preston, William, Jr. *Aliens and Dissenters*. Cambridge, Mass.: Harvard University Press, 1963.

Purcell, Victor. *The Chinese in Malaya*. New York: Oxford University Press, 1948.

Quigley, Harold S. *China's Politics in Perspective*. Minneapolis: The University of Minnesota Press, 1960.

Remer, C. F. *A Study of Chinese Boycott*. Baltimore: Johns Hopkins Press, 1933.

Riggs, Fred W. *Pressures on Congress: A Study of the Repeal of Chinese Exclusion*. New York: King's Crown Press, 1950.

Rosinger, Lawrence K. *China's Wartime Politics, 1937–1944*. Princeton: Princeton University Press, 1945.

Rubin, Charles. *The Log of Rubin the Sailor*. New York: International Publishers, 1973.

Sandmeyer, Elmer Clarence. *The Anti-Chinese Movement in California*. Chicago: University of Illinois Press, 1973.

Saxton, Alexander. *The Indispensible Enemy: Labor and the Anti-Chinese Movement in California*. Berkeley: University of California Press, 1971.

Schwartz, Shepherd. "The Chinese Community in New York City." Columbia University Research on Chinese Culture (CURCC), 1950.

Seldes, George. *Facts and Fascism*. New York: In Fact Inc., 1943.

Seward, George F. *Chinese Immigration in Its Social and Economic Aspects*. New York: Charles Scribner's, 1881.

Siu, Paul C. P. "The Chinese Laundrymen: A Study of Social Isolation." Ph.D. diss., University of Chicago, 1953.

Smedley, Agnes. *Battle Hymn of China*. New York: Alfred A. Knopf, 1943.

Soong, Ching Ling. *The Struggle for New China*. Peking: Foreign Language Press, 1952.

Spero, Sterling D. and Harris, Abram L. *The Black Worker*. New York: Atheneum Press, 1931.

Steele, A. T. *The American People and China*. New York: McGraw-Hill, 1966.

Sung, Betty Lee. *Mountain of Gold*. New York: MacMillan, 1967.

Terkel, Studs. *Hard Times: An Oral History of the Great Depression*. New York: Pantheon Books, 1970.

Thomas, John N. *The Institute of Pacific Relations: Asian Scholars and American Politics*. Seattle: University of Washington Press, 1974.

Tomasi, S. M. and Engels, Madline., eds. *Italian Experience in the United States*. New York: Center for Migration Studies, 1970.

Wales, Nym. *The Chinese Labor Movement*. New York: John Day Co., 1945.

Wu, Cheng Tsu. "Chinese People and Chinatown in New York City." Ph.D. diss., Clark University, 1958.

Young, Donald R. *American Minority People*. New York: Harper and Brothers, 1932.

Young, Marilyn Blatt. *American Expansionism: The Critical Issues*. Boston: Little Brown and Co., 1973.

INDEX